DISCOVERY SHIFT

Discovery Shift

*Why Talking Less
and Listening More
Wins Business*

CHRIS HOLMAN, MCC

horsesmouth®

NEW YORK

Disclaimer
This book is for educational purposes only and is not intended as financial, legal, or investment advice. Readers are advised to consult qualified financial, legal, or tax professionals before making any financial decisions.

Publisher's Cataloging-in-Publication Data
Holman, Chris, 1953–
Discovery Shift: Why Talking Less and Listening More Wins Business /
Chris Holman.—First edition.—New York: Horsesmouth, LLC, 2025.—
Includes index.

Identifiers:
LCCN 2025918556
ISBN 978-0-9767804-0-3 (softcover)

Subjects:
LCSH: Investment advisors. | Investment advisors and clients. | Financial planners—Marketing. | Financial planners—United States. | Business communication. | Listening—Psychological aspects.

Classification:
LCC HG179.5 .H65 2025 (print) | DDC 332.6/024—dc23

Ordering Information
Special discounts are available on quantity purchases by corporations, associations, and other organizations. For information contact:

Horsesmouth LLC
888-336-6884 (Outside the U.S.: 212-343-8760)
230 Park Avenue, 3rd Floor West
New York, NY 10169
horsesmouth.com
discovery-shift.com

10 9 8 7 6 5 4 3 2 1—Printed in the United States of America, 2025

Contents

PART ONE: Seeing the Problem Clearly

PART TWO: Understanding the Prospect's Reality

PART THREE: Designing a Trust-Centered Discovery Meeting

Preface

It started with a puzzle at a Horsesmouth Social Security training workshop in 2018. An advisor I met there had begun running his own workshops, for the purpose of educating and finding new clients. He was great at filling the room. And he was able to get a number of follow-up meetings. Yet not a single attendee had committed to becoming a client.

We began working together. In our first few coaching sessions, the pattern became clear. In discovery meetings, this advisor was physically imposing, with a bold, direct style that was overwhelming his prospects. Not intentionally, but unmistakably. His go-to move was interrogation-by-Why:

"Why do you own this?"
"Why do you have so much cash?"
"Why this?" "Why that?"

Once he recognized the impact of his tone and framing, he made a conscious shift. He softened his approach. Dropped the "why" questions. And sure enough, within a few months, he had his best revenue month ever. Credit to him for the awareness and the willingness to change.

When I shared his turnaround story with Sean Bailey, Horsesmouth's editor-in-chief, we both got curious: What really happens in a discovery meeting?

That question led to the creation of the Discovery Lab. We brought in actors to play prospective clients, recorded dozens of mock discovery meetings over Zoom, and studied the footage to see what patterns emerged. From there, we developed the Discovery Meeting workshops at Horsesmouth to share what we were learning.

Discovery Shift is the next evolution of that work, a deeper exploration into what makes a discovery conversation meaningful, memorable, and built for trust. For both advisor and prospect. We've come a long way since that first coaching session, but the central insight remains: discovery isn't a checklist. It's a shift in how we ask, how we listen, how we connect. This book is your invitation to make that shift your own, and to discover what happens when you do.

Acknowledgments

This book would not exist without the many advisors who stepped into the Discovery Lab and the Discovery Meeting workshops, sometimes bravely, sometimes skeptically, but always in good faith. Your conversations gave this work its shape. I've learned something from every one of you (even when it took me a while to realize it).

Thanks again to Sean Bailey, who did what good editors do: asked a simple question at the right moment, then gave the idea room to run. From the beginning, he's been acutely interested in what makes a good discovery meeting, and what doesn't.

To *The Refinement Guild:* Maxine, Julian, Tessa, and Frankie. Thank you for holding this work to a higher standard than I knew to aim for. Your precision, pushback, and quiet polish made this book not just better, but braver.

To my wife, Laurie Van Wieren, thank you for enduring an inordinate number of unsolicited writing updates, process musings, and random epithets from the other room. You never once asked me to stop. You may have *wanted* to, but you never did.

To my father, David Holman, who surrounded us with the love of reading and books from as long ago as I can remember, and who modeled the quiet curiosity that kept asking without ever needing to declare itself. Thank you, Dad.

And to my coach, Bobbi Gemma, whose steady presence and sharp questions and acute listening helped me keep the thinking clear and, in a coach-like way. You've been part of this project longer than anyone else, even before it had a name.

Introduction

No matter how long you've been in the business, discovery either moves the relationship forward, or quietly stalls it. Some advisors build it on instinct. Others inherit someone else's version and tweak it over time. Some don't think much about it at all. And some are ready to scale but know their current process won't get them there.

This book is for all of you.

It's not about scripts, closing tactics, or tricks to win fast trust. It's about a deeper shift: from transaction to transformation. From presenting to partnering. From *I ask, you answer*, to a shared conversation that builds clarity, safety, and momentum.

- If your discovery meetings feel too long, too flat, too shallow, or too inconsistent, this will help.
- If you're training others and want a structure that works, this will help.
- If your business is steady but growth has slowed, this will help.
- If you're in expansion mode and want to build trust at scale, this will help.

It's a fast read, but not a light one. Every chapter is designed to sharpen your awareness, deepen your presence, and shift the way you approach the most important conversation in your business. Read it straight through or skip to what you need. But read it. Because in a world full of noise, how you begin matters more than ever.

Discovery Shift is here to help you begin differently.

PART ONE

Seeing the Problem Clearly

We fall into patterns, especially in conversations we think we've mastered. You want to connect, to build trust, to serve. But even with good intentions, it's easy to miss cues, default to performance, or shut others down without realizing it.

This first part is an invitation to slow down and turn the mirror inward. To trace the habits you bring into discovery moments. The assumptions, defenses, and reflexes that shape how you listen and respond.

Trust starts with knowing yourself. These chapters help you catch what you've missed, question old habits, and shift how you engage.

Chapters in this section

- **The Blind Spot:** Why You're Not Hearing What You Think You Are

- **The Illusion of Transparency:** How Miscommunication Silently Erodes Trust

- **What Are We Really Saying?** Rethinking the Language of Discovery

- **The Habit Loop of Over-Talking:** Why Familiar Patterns Hold You Back

- **Breaking the Cycle of Conversational Dominance:** Creating Space for True Connection

- **The Comfort Trap:** Why Change Feels Hard, and How to Make it Stick

1

THE BLIND SPOT

Why You're Not Seeing What You Think You Are

When positive signals lead you astray

Malcolm thought the meeting had gone well. He greeted the couple warmly, walked them through his process, even shared a personal story about his father's retirement that usually earned a smile. They nodded in all the right places and said what every advisor wants to hear: "This was really helpful."

Malcolm logged off the Zoom call feeling good. Confident. Certain he'd made a strong impression. But the follow-up email went unanswered. So did the one after that. Eventually, silence. He chalked it up to timing. Maybe they weren't ready. Maybe they were shopping around. What Malcolm never considered is what many advisors, seasoned, skilled, well-meaning advisors, overlook every day. Maybe it wasn't the prospect. Maybe it was the conversation.

The accidental process

Advisors spend years sharpening technical skills. They build plans, model scenarios, and stay current on markets and tax codes. But when it comes to discovery, the part that often matters most, the process usually isn't designed. It's formed, repeated, and reinforced. Ask advisors how they approach discovery, and you'll often hear:

"It depends on the prospect."
"Every meeting is different."
"It's evolved over time."

Flexibility matters. Still, there's a fine line between being adaptive and being automatic. Over time, the approach starts to feel comfortable. Familiar. And familiarity tends to feel like mastery. But without real feedback, it's hard to tell what's actually working and what's simply habit. When success is measured by whether a prospect says "yes," there's little insight into the quality of the conversation itself. No one tells you when the prospect left feeling misunderstood. No one points out that you missed their most important concern. No one highlights the moment they mentally checked out but kept nodding politely.

And so the pattern continues. And this is the blind spot. These blind spots don't announce themselves. Advisors don't realize what they're missing until something jars them, like listening back to a meeting they thought went well. The gap between intention and impact is often wider than it feels.

What the Discovery Lab reveals

At the Horsesmouth Discovery Lab, we recorded and analyzed nearly 100 discovery meetings with financial advisors. These weren't real prospect meetings. They were structured role-plays with professional actors playing prospective clients. What made them powerful was how real they felt. Advisors showed up as they normally would: improvising, presenting, reacting.

Because every conversation was recorded and reviewed for key behaviors, we could see what advisors typically miss. And the data is sobering:

- Advisors dominate the conversation, speaking nearly 70 percent of the time.
- Most questions are fact-based, close-ended, or overly scripted.
- Key emotional cues often go unnoticed.
- Many advisors think they're building rapport, when they may actually be creating polite disengagement.

Here's what that disconnect can look like in practice: The advisor walks through their recommendation, clear, confident, and data-backed. The prospect nods along, offering polite affirmations. Everything appears to be going well. But beneath the surface, something crucial is missing. The advisor hasn't paused to ask what the prospect is actually worried about. There's no space for the client's story, no cue that their emotions matter. What sounds like a productive exchange is in reality a quiet miss.

This isn't a failure of effort, or intellect. It's the residue of old habits. Habits that once signaled competence but now mute the very signals that matter.

This isn't a new script

The goal of Discovery Shift isn't to replace one script with another. It's not about memorizing better questions or simply talking less. It's about noticing what's easy to miss when you've been doing this a while. You might be great at financial planning. You might be terrific at client service. But your discovery process? That part might be bland, or mediocre, or worse. And if it is, you're not alone.

What great discovery really looks like

If we no longer measure discovery by whether someone "closes," then what do we measure instead? That's a fair question. And it deserves a better answer than the industry usually gives. Here are a few signs that a discovery meeting is doing real work:

- The prospect says something they've never shared before.
- Rather than reacting, they pause, reflect, and engage.
- They talk more than you do.
- You help uncover the emotional truth beneath the financial concern.
- They feel seen, not sized up.
- They express a desire to continue the conversation without being asked.
- You walk away knowing you offered real help, not a sales pitch.

These aren't gimmicks. They're the natural outcomes of a conversation built on connection, curiosity, and intentional design. Throughout this book, we'll explore benchmarks like these. Not the binary "Did I close?" outcomes, but deeper signals of clarity, engagement, and trust.

Beyond the close

Let's be clear. We're not suggesting you abandon the business goals of discovery meetings. Yes, they're about growth. About bringing in new clients. About building something meaningful and profitable.

But the way to get there isn't through pressure or performance. When you stop trying to win every prospect, you show up more naturally, more curiously, more authentically. And in that space, you connect with the people who truly resonate. The ones most likely to trust, stay, and refer. In other words, when you stop chasing the close, you build a better business. And while that may sound contrary to what many advisors have been taught, there's solid research, and real-world psychology, to back it up.

*A **note on performance**: In this book, when we talk about "performance," we don't mean job performance. We mean performing a role instead of showing up as your genuine self. It is acting like the "ideal" advisor, doing what looks competent or polished, and chasing approval instead of connection. Performance lives in habit and showmanship, not in curiosity, courage, or care. It is the mask that keeps an advisor safe but forgettable.*

Why "stop chasing the close" is backed by science

It might feel counterintuitive, letting go of the instinct to "close" every prospect. After all, traditional sales training often frames closing techniques as the ultimate mark of success.

But empirical research tells a different story. A study in the *Journal of Personal Selling & Sales Management* found that high-pressure closing tactics can actually erode credibility, a critical ingredient in lasting client relationships. Psychologist Robert Cialdini, in *Influence: Science and Practice,* reinforces this: real commitment stems from trust and understanding, not persuasion. Modern sales psychology agrees. The more advisors focus on building trust rather than forcing decisions, the more naturally prospects move forward.

Here's the irony: The less you try to close, the more you create an environment where prospects feel relaxed, understood, and genuinely engaged. And that's what ultimately grows a stronger business.

Reconstructing your discovery meetings begins here

Before we go further, let's clarify what this book is about. It's a call to reimagine how you connect, both with your prospects and with yourself. The real magic of discovery is how little it needs to impress to make an impact. Discovery meetings are about creating a space where people can speak freely, without pretense or pressure.

That kind of conversation doesn't happen by accident. It's built intentionally: designed, practiced, revisited. Fueled by empathy, guided by curiosity, anchored in purpose. That's the ethos behind this book. We want to challenge the idea that discovery is merely a step in the sales process. It's a discipline, a mindset, a way of showing up.

And it starts by seeing what many advisors miss. To lead discovery well, you have to notice what you're listening for, how you're reacting, and what you're choosing to follow. What begins as a method for guiding others often becomes a way of reorienting yourself.

Take a moment. Set aside your assumptions. Let go of how you may imagine discovery is supposed to go. What comes next is a chance to rethink how discovery really works, so it stops feeling like a sales spiel and starts becoming a conversation worth having. Conversations that not only engage your prospects but reshape how you see your role entirely. This is where the shift begins.

2
THE ILLUSION OF TRANSPARENCY

How Miscommunication Silently Erodes Trust

You think you're being clear. You're not.

In discovery meetings, many advisors believe they're building trust by sharing stories, explaining their process, and listening for cues. But a hidden bias quietly undercuts their efforts: the illusion of transparency. We assume our meaning is arriving intact, unfiltered, understood. That prospects don't simply hear what we said. They get what we meant. In truth, what feels clear to us can feel confusing or disconnected to them. And because few prospects speak up when something misses the mark, the gap quietly grows.

The bias you can't see

In *The Blind Spot*, we explored how discovery conversations often run on autopilot, shaped more by habit than intention. But even when advisors are intentional, another hidden challenge remains: the gap between what they think they're communicating and what prospects actually hear.

Most advisors believe they're clearer, more engaging, and better listeners than they actually are. Not out of carelessness, but because they're human. A quiet cognitive bias is at play. Behavioral scientists and psychologists call it the "illusion of transparency": the belief that our thoughts and intentions are coming across exactly as we mean them, that the person across the table or screen truly understands what we meant, beyond the words we used. The illusion stems from how acutely we experience our own thoughts and emotions. We assume others can easily pick up on the same cues, when in fact they often don't. It's a distortion fueled by egocentric bias, where we anchor on our own perspective and fail to modify for how little others actually know or perceive. But what we think we're communicating and what the listener actually hears are often two very different things.

A conversation gap you didn't know existed

Imagine explaining something important on a Zoom call, only to realize later you were on mute the entire time. You thought your message landed, but no one heard a word. This is what happens in prospect conversations more often than we think. We assume we've been clear, but the signal gets lost somewhere in transmission. Research in psychology and communication confirms the pattern: speakers believe they've been understood, listeners hesitate to admit confusion, and both walk away thinking they're aligned, even when they're not. It's not carelessness. It's human nature. But in financial advising, where clarity and trust are nonnegotiable, this gap can have real consequences.

The illusion of connection

We've recorded and listened to scores of discovery meetings. Advisors often believed their meetings went well. But when we reviewed the recordings, a different story surfaced:

- They thought they were asking deep questions, but most stayed surface-level.
- They believed they were building connection. They missed subtle emotional cues.
- They assumed prospects understood, but many left unclear or unengaged.

No one told them they'd missed the mark. So the illusion persisted. These weren't bad advisors. They were capable professionals working under a false sense of certainty.

Why good intentions aren't enough

One reason the illusion of transparency is so persistent is that it feels logical. If something makes sense to us, we assume it must make sense to others. But communication doesn't work that way. Advisors often fall into subtle traps, talking too much, convinced they're being clear; sharing stories that don't quite land; or assuming they know what the prospect wants without actually checking. We believe the message got through, unaware the conversation may have already drifted off course.

Have you ever been in a conversation where you weren't fully following, but didn't say so? Maybe you were disinterested. Maybe you didn't want to interrupt. Maybe you were too embarrassed to ask. That's another face of the illusion of transparency. But from the other side of the table.

Slowing down the assumptions

For advisors, the solution isn't to talk more or explain harder. It's to slow down and check in. Gently. Curiously. Without assuming alignment. You might ask, "How does that land with you?" or "What are you thinking as you hear this?" These small invitations open the door for real feedback, especially when paired with attentive listening. Hesitations, vague responses, and clipped answers may seem minor, but they often signal a deeper disconnect. Even when the conversation appears to be going well on the surface, these cues suggest the prospect is following but not fully engaging.

Awareness is a skill

You can't eliminate the illusion of transparency. But you can train yourself to notice it. You can reflect after meetings:

- Did I check in enough?
- Was I truly listening?
- Did I invite the prospect to share openly, or was I too focused on (over) explaining things clearly (or what I thought was clear)?

You can even review your own conversations; by recording them, role-playing, or jotting notes afterward. And you hear what's said, as well as what's left unsaid.

Where honesty begins

A prospect's most honest moment rarely comes at the beginning of a conversation. It often emerges later, after a pause, a question, or a moment when the advisor simply holds the silence without rushing to fill it. What makes that moment possible isn't charisma or technical fluency. It's presence. The kind that makes uncertainty feel welcome.

Sometimes you think you've been clear. Until you notice the hesitation in their eyes, the polite nod, the sideways question that doesn't quite track. That's not a failure. It's a signal. A chance to slow down, to ask, to listen for what landed and what didn't. Clarity is a shared effort. Clarity takes shape in the space between what's said and what's still unheard.

Thoughts to carry forward

Breaking the illusion begins with one shift: recognizing that you are not the best judge of how well you're communicating. Three ways to close the gap:

1. Test for clarity. Don't assume prospects understood. Ask them. Try: "Am I tracking with you so far?" Or "What part of that stands out to you?"
2. Watch for nonverbal clues. If someone grows quiet, don't assume it's agreement. It might be confusion or disengagement.
3. Create space. If you're talking more than 50% of the time, pause. Make room for what the prospect needs to say, even more than what you want to share.

3

WHAT ARE WE REALLY SAYING?

Rethinking the Language of Discovery

Why words matter in Discovery

In discovery meetings, language sets the frame. It guides what we notice, how we interpret it, and what actions feel possible. It nudges behavior, frames intent, and signals whose experience is being prioritized. And in the financial advice industry, a lot of the default language reveals something we don't always want to admit. We're often still talking like salespeople.

Take the term "pain points." It shows up everywhere: in new advisor training, in advisors' vocabulary, and on whiteboards during Monday meetings. The idea is simple. Identify what's not working in a prospect's life, then present the fix. Locate the pain, offer the pill.

It's not that people don't experience real financial stress or uncertainty. They do. But framing those experiences as *pain points* subtly shifts the tone of the interaction. It nudges the advisor into a role that's more strategic than relational, someone looking for leverage, not understanding. The client becomes less of a person, more of a case. Even if your intentions are good, the language leans sales-first. It treats human complexity like a conversion opportunity.

What's the alternative? Start with better questions, and better framing. Ask what feels unresolved. Explore where they feel stuck. Listen for emotional drivers instead of fishing for vulnerabilities. When you do that well, people don't feel *closed*. They feel understood.

Another term worth exploring is "prospect"

This one's trickier. It's useful. Every advisor knows what it means. It creates definition, someone is either a client or a prospect. And there's nothing inherently wrong with the word in operational terms. But in conversation? In mindset? It comes with baggage.

When we think of someone as a "prospect," we subtly shift into a sales posture. We look for conversion signals. We measure engagement against closing probabilities. We enter the meeting hoping they'll become something for us: a client, a source of revenue, a notch on the growth chart. But people don't want to feel prospected. Like gold in the foothills of the Sierra Nevadas. They want to feel seen. They want to know this goes beyond onboarding. It's about being heard, being helped, and being taken seriously.

That said, we're going to use the word "prospect" throughout this book. It's clear, it's efficient, and it keeps the language consistent. But let's not sleepwalk through it. I invite all of us to become hyper-aware of the words we choose and the behaviors they promote. Language not only reflects our thinking, it shapes it. And the discovery meeting deserves better than autopilot vocabulary.

If we're not careful, the term "prospect" turns the discovery meeting into a scripted play. The advisor asks the standard questions. The prospect gives the expected answers. Everyone plays their part, and nothing real gets said. This goes beyond word choice. Language shapes behavior, as any good training designer or behavioral scientist will tell you. We see it in other common terms that show up in training materials and CRM dashboards: pipeline, objections, scripts, conversion rate. All of it sounds like machinery. And all of it trains the advisor to think in steps, not in people.

Of course, businesses need structure. Pipelines aren't going away. But behind the scenes, and especially in client-facing language, we have to be more careful. We have to ask whether the words we're using are shaping us into the kind of advisors we actually want to be.

Rewriting the script

Here's what better language sounds like:

- Instead of "qualify the prospect," try "understand where they're at."
- Instead of "pain points," try "unmet needs" or "unspoken worries."
- Instead of "overcoming objections," try "helping them wrestle with their questions."
- Instead of "move them down the funnel," try "build simplicity at each step."

None of these are euphemisms. They're clearer. They're more honest. They encourage a mindset that values the relationship over tactics.

And that matters. Because there's a business case here too. A strong one.

Advisors who use emotionally intelligent, human-centered language in discovery meetings build trust faster. Real trust leads to stronger relationships, lasting engagement, and more introductions. Clients say yes more readily when the meeting brings insight instead of pressure. They stay with you because the relationship feels aligned, not engineered. And they refer others not because the advisor dazzled them, but because the experience felt honest, thoughtful, and real.

If you're training others in discovery, this matters even more. Language affects behavior. The right words lead to better questions, better listening, and more confidence. And if you're building a brand, those words become part of your culture.

Discovery is more than a fact-finding mission. It's the emotional ignition point of the relationship. If you get the tone right there, everything that follows is easier. Trust builds faster. Advice lands more cleanly. Referrals follow. In the end, people don't remember your process. They walk away remembering the emotional tone, not the technical details. The words you use will either support that feeling or get in the way of it. Language is leverage. If we want discovery to feel like a partnership, our words have to do that work too.

Thoughts to carry forward

1. The language used in discovery meetings subtly shapes behavior, framing the advisor's mindset and influencing how clients are perceived and engaged.
2. Sales-heavy terms like "pain points" and "prospect" reinforce transactional dynamics, whereas more human-centered language fosters trust and genuine connection.
3. Emotionally intelligent language strengthens discovery outcomes by building trust, deepening engagement, and making the experience feel more aligned and authentic.

4

THE HABIT LOOP
OF OVER-TALKING

Why Familiar Patterns Hold You Back

How good intentions become self-sabotage

The conversation might feel smooth, even productive. But if you're the one doing most of the talking, connection isn't happening. It's habit. A neurological one. And until you interrupt that reflex, real discovery stays out of reach.

Why do good advisors, smart, experienced, well-intentioned advisors, still talk more than they should?

It's not arrogance. It's not carelessness. And it's not a lack of self-awareness. It's habit; a deeply ingrained reflex, reinforced over years of prospect meetings, calls, and presentations.

You've likely felt it yourself: the pressure to fill silence, the urge to prove your value, the instinct to explain more. And before you know it, you're doing most of the talking, maybe even two-thirds of it. Many advisors spot the pattern too late, after the call ends and they realize how little they heard.

Over-talking follows a neurological script

The human brain is built for efficiency. Once a pattern is repeated enough, it runs on its own. That's why we don't have to think about tying our shoes or riding a bike. The behavior automatically takes over. Every habit runs on a loop:

- **Cue:** A trigger, like silence or the pressure to prove yourself
- **Routine:** The automatic behavior, i.e., more words and more explaining
- **Reward:** A momentary feeling of control, connection, or relief

Neuroscientists call this long-term potentiation (LTP): the process by which repeated behaviors strengthen neural pathways, making them easier to repeat. Each time a prospect nods or lets you keep talking, your brain gets a small reward, a hit of dopamine. It learns: This works. Do it again.

The irony? What feels good to you, such as talking, elaborating, and reassuring, often feels overwhelming to the person across the table.

Discovery facts

Across nearly 100 recorded role-play sessions, one pattern stood out: advisors consistently dominated the conversation. The key insight is the extent of the imbalance, how much more advisors talked, and how widely it varied across individuals. That range tells us this isn't an isolated issue. It's systemic:

- The most talkative advisors spoke 85% of the time
- Even the most concise spoke 52%
- No one spoke less than half the time
- In some meetings, advisors spoke seven times more than the prospect

The role of the brain in habit formation

Two key areas of the brain govern our habits. The **basal ganglia** stores habitual behaviors and runs them on autopilot. Once a behavior is encoded here, it plays out below conscious awareness. In contrast, the **prefrontal cortex** is responsible for deliberate thought and self-regulation. That moment when an advisor pauses to listen rather than respond is the prefrontal cortex at work, and it takes effort.

Meanwhile, talking lights up the brain's reward system. A Harvard study found that speaking about oneself activates the brain's pleasure centers, much like food, money, or social praise. That hit of affirmation feels good, chemically satisfying. And that's exactly why the loop keeps repeating.

Why over-talking becomes automatic

Over-talking doesn't happen because advisors lack self-awareness. What happens is that once a behavior is repeated enough, the brain locks it in. Neural pathways get wrapped in myelin, making them faster and more efficient, like laying down a track for a reflex. The brain craves cognitive efficiency, preferring low-energy, familiar actions, like talking, over higher-effort ones, like pausing or sitting with uncertainty. And then there's the social layer: silence is often misread as awkward, even disengaged. Many advisors have been conditioned to equate speaking with clarity and competence. But in reality, silence, used intentionally, is one of the most powerful tools for building trust.

The challenge of rewiring a habit

The good news? The brain is adaptable. It's called neuroplasticity, the ability to form new neural pathways and weaken old ones. But this takes more than awareness. It takes intentional effort. You don't have to impress prospects to earn their trust. You simply have to meet them where they are.

Awareness isn't enough. Intentionality is essential.

Awareness is a starting point, but it's not enough. Change doesn't happen automatically because someone realizes they tend to over-talk. It happens when they choose to do something about it. Not someday. Not casually. They commit to talking less, listening more, and doing the real work of behavior change. That doesn't mean reading another book or signing up for another workshop. It means practicing new habits, asking for feedback, and reflecting on how they actually show up.

Over-talking might be unconscious but change never is. It takes recognition: *I talk more than I think I do.* It takes intention: *I want to shift that.* And it takes practice: *I pause, ask, and listen on purpose.* That's why most people don't change. And it's exactly why you can, if you choose to be intentional.

The identity shift behind breaking the habit

Talking, for many advisors, is more than a behavior. It's a core part of how they show value and steer conversations, so pulling back can feel disorienting. But talking less doesn't mean being less. It means making room for more. More openness, more truth, more connection. The hardest habits to break are often the ones that made us successful. But every time you resist the urge to speak, you make space for something rare: true connection. That's the kind of discovery that stays with someone. It creates clarity, builds trust, and opens the door to something real.

Thoughts to carry forward

1. What looks like over-talking is often a reflex, shaped by habitual patterns and reinforced over time.
2. Real change challenges both behavior and identity.
3. And it starts with choosing, deliberately and consistently, to show up differently in conversation.

5

BREAKING THE CYCLE
OF CONVERSATIONAL
DOMINANCE

Creating Space for True Connection

The unintended habit

Most advisors don't mean to dominate conversations. It happens almost unintentionally. They begin with good intentions: explaining, answering, proving their value. Minutes pass. They're still the only ones talking. The prospect has barely said a word. The meeting drifts from dialogue into monologue.

This response pattern didn't appear out of nowhere. It developed over time, shaped by training, social expectations, and the emotional signals we pick up in high-stakes conversations. Like any habit, it can be unlearned. But noticing it is only the starting point. Shifting from over-talking to dialogue requires deliberate effort.

Why we talk too much

Over the course of nearly 100 role-played discovery meetings, a clear pattern emerged: advisors talked more than 70% of the time. That's not a conversation. It's a stage. Why does it happen?

- **Pressure to perform:** You want to prove you're capable, so you lean into what you know.
- **Fear of silence:** Empty space feels awkward, so you fill it.
- **Genuine excitement:** You're passionate about helping, so you explain, often for too long.

These moments aren't malicious, but when left unchecked, they erode trust and limit connection.

The power of intentional silence

Some conversations only deepen when there's space. Space that's unrushed, unfilled, and genuinely open. That's when people start to reflect, respond, and feel truly heard. Intentional silence, used well, becomes more than a pause. It becomes a tool for trust. But to use it skillfully, advisors need to be aware of their own habits. Are you jumping in to rescue a pause? Repeating yourself, solely to be sure? Are you watching the prospect's pacing and body language. Or are you driving the meeting like a scripted tour? Silence isn't absence. It's an invitation. And when the space feels collaborative, buy-in follows naturally.

Setting the stage for self-awareness

Before we go further, let's pause on a subtle but foundational idea. We explore this in detail in future chapters, but here's the quick version: When people meet someone new, they assess two things, warmth and competence. It happens in milliseconds. These impressions shape how safe someone feels speaking freely.

Even when an advisor appears warm, subtle dynamics; like who controls the topic, who speaks the longest, and who is interrupted, can undermine that warmth. This pattern is especially pronounced for women, whose voices, culturally speaking, have long been treated as less authoritative. In our Discovery Lab recordings, advisors spoke about 70% of the time (as we've noted previously). Of the remaining 30%, male prospects accounted for roughly 20%, while female prospects averaged only 10%. The numbers reveal how easily conversational space can tilt, even in seemingly positive interactions.

Cultural conditioning and conversational habits

Awareness begins when we slow down enough to notice what's really happening, beneath the words and beyond the habits. Decades of research show that men are more likely to interrupt, steer conversations toward their own topics, and dominate speaking time, especially in mixed-gender settings. These aren't conscious choices. They're cultural defaults.

For advisors, many of whom are men, talking less marks a deeper shift, an act of unlearning. Common patterns of conversational dominance include:

- **Quantitative dominance:** speaking for longer or using more words
- **Participatory dominance:** interrupting or overlapping another speaker
- **Sequential dominance:** steering the flow and direction of the conversation

These behaviors aren't about gender identity alone. They're shaped by habit, training, and context. Still, the cultural pattern matters.

Notably, there are exceptions to these generalizations. For example, in our Discovery Lab observations, the advisor who demonstrated the least conversational dominance was male. Also, every female advisor we recorded spoke for more than 50 percent of the meeting.

Here's how conversational dominance can play out. An advisor, eager to help, speaks confidently. He explains thoroughly, follows a structured set of questions, and believes he's guiding the conversation well. But if he isn't attuned to balance, he may be controlling the experience; setting the agenda, defining the rhythm, and signaling whose input carries more weight. Meanwhile, the prospect across the table nods, listens, smiles. But she may be disengaging. Not because she doesn't care, but because she doesn't feel invited in. That's when relationships quietly start to unravel.

Women now control more wealth than ever and are leading more financial decisions, often as equal or primary decision-makers in their households. Yet too many discovery conversations still miss the mark. If a woman (or any prospect) leaves a meeting feeling unheard, there likely won't be a second meeting.

Practical strategies for talking less and listening more

Shifting from monologue to dialogue takes effort. These strategies help:

1. **The Sixty-Second Rule:** After answering a question or making a point, pause and let the prospect respond. Ask yourself: Have I spoken for more than 60 seconds? If so, stop. Redirect the conversation.
2. **The Three-Second Rule:** Pausing before responding signals thoughtfulness. Ask a question. Then count to three before speaking again.
3. **Active listening and paraphrasing:** Reflect what you've heard: "It sounds like your biggest concern is not running out of money in retirement. Did I get that right?"
4. **Replace statements with questions:** Instead of: "You need a diversified portfolio." Try: "What's shaped your view on investing?" Instead of: "Do you have a retirement plan?" Try: "What does retirement look like to you?"
5. **Use "Tell me more":** A simple invitation that unlocks insight. "That's interesting. Tell me more." And "What led you to that conclusion?"

Recognizing disengagement

Disengagement rarely announces itself. It shows up in quieter forms, such as passive agreement, unanswered questions, or the absence of emotional language. These signals are easy to misread as signs of satisfaction, but more often they point to disconnection.

When you sense the energy shift, pause and reset. Try saying, "I'm sorry. I realize that I've been talking for a while now. I want to make sure I'm not getting ahead of you. What's coming up for you as we've been talking?" Or, "We've covered a lot, but I haven't heard much from you yet. What's important that we haven't gotten to?" Self-awareness in moments like these carries more weight than any chart or credential ever will.

The business impact of talking less

Advisors who listen more than they speak build deeper trust and stronger relationships. Neuroscience, behavioral research, and Discovery Lab data all support this. Solid evidence, not isolated stories. Here's the practical argument: when clients feel heard, they stay. They follow your guidance, refer others, and remain loyal.

Discovery meetings work best when the focus stays on the other person, their values, their concerns, and the context behind their decisions. That's where real connection starts.

Thoughts to carry forward

Great advisors know how to create room for others to speak fully. They listen with intention, respond with care, and let the conversation unfold on the prospect's terms. That's what builds trust. Try these small experiments in your next meeting:

1. Track your talk-to-listen ratio. Aim for 50/50 or better.
2. Practice the three-second rule. Wait when you want to jump in.
3. Use "Tell me more." See where it leads.

6

THE COMFORT TRAP

Why Change Feels Hard, and How to Make It Stick

The paradox of knowing but not changing

You know the drill. You spot the pattern, try a new habit, maybe even see some progress. Then? Backslide. Why is lasting change so slippery?

Most advisors want to evolve. They study best practices, attend trainings, and hear all the right advice: listen more, build trust, go deeper. Yet when it comes time to actually change their approach, many don't. The resistance isn't about knowledge. Advisors understand what needs to change. Implementing it is another story. What holds them back often stems from how they think about the work. And what they know.

The financial services industry rewards competence, expertise, and control. Advisors spend years mastering complex financial strategies, staying current on regulations, and delivering confident answers. That creates tension. On one hand, they might recognize the need to shift their approach in discovery meetings. On the other, change feels risky, uncomfortable, even unnecessary, especially for those with a solid track record. Understanding why change feels hard is the first step to making it happen.

Expertise and the illusion of certainty

Advisors are trained to be experts. Prospects expect clarity and confidence. This creates a powerful trap: the belief that "I already know this." Overconfidence bias leads advisors to assume their current approach is working well enough. As we've seen in our Discovery Lab, many don't realize how much they dominate conversations, until they watch themselves back. The shock isn't in what they hear. It's in what they missed. Change isn't about admitting failure. It's about seeing clearly enough to grow. The best advisors understand that expertise isn't static. It evolves.

The comfort zone problem

Familiarity feels safe, even when it's ineffective. When advisors repeat the same approach for years, change can feel like a risk. The brain resists disruption and defaults to what's easy and familiar. That's why some still rush rapport, over-explain, or lean too hard on fact-finding. These patterns feel safer, even when they don't work.

The comfort trap is strongest when the old approach still "works." If clients are coming in, why fix it? But client expectations evolve. What worked yesterday may not work tomorrow. Even with the right tools, old habits resurface, especially under pressure. That's why change must be deliberate. Left on autopilot, we slide back into comfort.

Discomfort doesn't mean something's gone wrong. It often marks the edge of your current capacity, the place where growth starts. Top advisors recognize that edge and keep moving through it.

Vulnerability is not weakness

Discovery requires presence, openness, and emotional engagement. That can feel risky. Some advisors resist change because it means giving up control. Asking deeper questions, allowing silence, or admitting uncertainty may feel like a loss of authority. But prospects don't expect perfection. They expect authenticity.

Ironically, the more advisors try to project total control, the less resonance their words carry. Prospects want to feel understood, not managed. The best discovery meetings happen when advisors listen deeply and respond in real time, not when they follow a script. Prospects trust real people, not polished presentations. Pausing, asking, and truly listening shows confidence, not weakness.

Discovery opens relationships while gathering facts along the way

Very often, advisors treat discovery as a way to extract facts and showcase expertise. That approach misses the point. What actually moves a conversation forward is the sense that the prospect feels seen and heard. The facts still matter, but they're only useful if the other person feels safe enough to share them fully. When advisors treat discovery as an invitation to connect, their behavior shifts. They ask more open-ended questions, allow silence, and respond to what's actually being said, even when it defies their expectations.

Discomfort is the growth signal

Advisors often assume discomfort means something's wrong. But discomfort is a hallmark of growth. Think of any real breakthrough: taking the CFP® exam, leading a first client meeting, having a hard conversation. None of those felt easy. But each moved you forward.

Discovery works the same way. Asking a personal question might feel awkward. Letting silence linger might create anxiousness. But those moments often spark the biggest shifts. The best advisors don't wait for comfort. They walk straight into the hard parts.

The habit of improvement

The most effective advisors are the ones still sharpening their skills. They actively seek feedback, review their meetings, and invest time in coaching and role-play. Growth is part of their routine. It's a discipline they keep alive.

Improvement begins with a single mindset shift, followed by a single step forward. Advisors who evolve keep a close eye on their own habits, approaching them with curiosity and a willingness to refine. Polish comes second to participation. Advisors who lean into growth signal their readiness to level up, not because they were off track, but because they're aiming higher.

Tactics for turning awareness into change

If awareness is the first step, what comes next is equally important: reflection, feedback, and behavior adjustment. These aren't abstract ideals. They're specific habits that help advisors close the gap between how they think they're showing up and how they're actually experienced.

1. **Self-audit:** After your next three discovery meetings, jot down:

- One moment where you felt completely in control
- One moment where you felt slightly uncomfortable

Then ask yourself: "Did that uncomfortable moment lead to deeper engagement?" If yes, how can you create more of those moments in the future? Small, consistent adaptations are what drive real change.

2. **Post-meeting reflection:** Make it a habit to check in with yourself:

- Did I interrupt the prospect?
- Did I ask more open-ended or closed-ended questions?
- Did I speak more than I listened?
- Did I leave space for emotional or personal sharing?

3. **Record and review your meetings:** The fastest way to spot blind spots is to hear yourself. If you're speaking more than 60–70% of the time, that's not discovery. It's a performance. Track your talk-time. Listen for tone, pacing, and the kinds of questions you ask.

4. **Role-play and peer feedback:** Have a trusted peer observe you in a role-play. Ask them to flag moments when you:

- Jumped in too quickly
- Missed an emotional cue
- Defaulted to explanation instead of curiosity

5. **The three-second pause:** Train yourself to pause for three full seconds after a prospect finishes speaking. This one habit changes everything. It prevents you from rushing in, creates space for deeper reflection, and often prompts the prospect to keep talking.

6. **Client feedback loops:** After a discovery meeting, try a simple ask: "What stood out to you today?" or "Did you feel heard?" Their responses hint at how connected, or distant, you felt to them.

These aren't gimmicks. They're micro-habits that compound into lasting change. And they anchor a broader shift: from leading with expertise to leading with awareness. That's the real work of discovery, and the path toward truly transformative conversations.

Thoughts to carry forward

1. Change stalls when comfort and overconfidence override self-awareness.
2. Discovery improves when advisors trade control for presence and trust.
3. Growth sticks through habits like reflection, feedback, and deeper listening

PART TWO

Understanding the Prospect's Reality

You've done the work to see yourself more clearly. Now it's time to cross the table. Prospects don't show up as blank slates. They arrive carrying emotion, hesitation, mental overload, and fears they often can't name. If you're only listening for facts, you'll miss what really matters. This section helps you tune into the emotional undercurrent: the trust signals, the quiet resistance, the fear of making the wrong move. To build connection, you have to feel what they feel.

Chapters in this section

- **The Psychology of Trust:** Why Prospects Feel It Before They Think It
- **Decision Fatigue and Cognitive Load:** Helping Prospects Navigate Overwhelm
- **Navigating Difficult Prospect Emotions:** Turning Tension Into Opportunity
- **What They're Not Saying:** Reading the Subtle Cues
- **Loss Aversion and the Fear of Change:** Understanding What Really Drives Decisions
- **The Hidden Truth:** Why Prospects Don't Always Tell You Everything

7

THE PSYCHOLOGY
OF TRUST

Why Prospects Feel It Before They Think It

Trust is a feeling, not a fact

Ask a roomful of advisors how they build trust, and you'll hear a list of rational proof points: credentials, experience, transparency, a well-defined process. All valid. But none of those things, on their own, create the emotional experience of trust.

Trust doesn't start with a decision. It starts as a feeling. Often subtle, sometimes immediate, always physical. The body picks up on safety, presence, and attention long before the brain catches up.

In a discovery meeting, prospects are asking themselves questions they'll never say out loud. Do I feel safe with this person? Can I be honest with them? Will they judge me? Are they really here with me, or simply performing something they've rehearsed? These are emotional assessments, not intellectual ones. And they happen fast. Social psychologists call this "thin-slicing"; our ability to make quick, often unconscious judgments based on very limited information. Within the first minute or two, your prospect is sizing you up, who you are, how you carry yourself, not only what you know. Are you warm? Are you attuned? Do you seem sincere?

Research shows that we tend to judge others on two traits: warmth and competence. But warmth comes first. If someone seems guarded or self-promoting, we often tune out before we notice how capable they are. That's especially true in advisory work. Leading with credentials or product knowledge, before establishing connection, can backfire. People need to feel safe before they can engage with expertise.

Trust forms fast. Not through argument or evidence, but through emotion. It settles in when something lands, when the other person feels seen or heard in a way that resonates beyond words. You either create safety and openness, or you don't. And if you don't, the prospect may nod along, say thank you, and never come back.

The trust timeline: how prospects decide in real time

Trust doesn't unfold evenly. It builds, or dissolves, in moments. Advisors often think of discovery meetings as a slow, steady process. But prospects experience them as a sequence of emotional cues. In every small moment, they're wondering, consciously or not, if you're someone they can rely on.

In the first two minutes, you're not evaluated for your financial knowledge. People pick up on your energy, your tone, and how fully you show up. Body language, eye contact, vocal tone, even how you settle into your chair, these shape the first impression. People are scanning for signs of safety. Do you seem calm, warm, engaged? These instincts are ancient and automatic, even if we're unaware of them.

By minute fifteen, the emotional tone starts to settle. If the advisor is too quick to lead, too eager to explain, or too focused on collecting facts, the prospect may hold back. But when the advisor is curious, listens fully, and allows silence, something shifts. The prospect begins to lean in. Trust takes root, not through expertise, but empathy. Discovery opens when you're fully there. When your attention lands and your tone signals safety, something shifts. The prospect can feel it. Attention settles, tension drops, and a different kind of conversation becomes possible.

Midway through, if trust has begun to form, prospects may start sharing things they didn't plan to reveal. Financial concerns that sound a lot like personal fears. Life transitions that carry emotional weight. These are the moments that turn a generic meeting into a real relationship. And yet, this is where many advisors blow it. They hear something meaningful and jump to fix it. Advice takes over. The prospect, just beginning to feel safe, suddenly feels managed. Trust stalls. The middle of the discovery conversation isn't for solving. It's for listening, reflecting, creating space for the prospect to feel heard and understood.

The final moments matter. They can reinforce trust or quietly unravel it. A clear summary, a thoughtful reflection, and a simple explanation of next steps can do more to build confidence than a perfect pitch. Prospects remember how they felt at the end. If the closing is rushed, vague, or transactional, it leaves a residue of uncertainty. But when it ends with clarity and care, the final message is unmistakable: I see you. I understand what matters to you. And I'm prepared to help.

The financial plan fallacy

Many advisors, especially those trained as planners, carry an unspoken assumption: once the plan is clear, the prospect will feel better. It's a comforting idea. Logical. Orderly. Clean. But human behavior isn't clean. A plan doesn't resolve emotional weight. It doesn't automatically build trust. And it rarely addresses the quiet fears hiding beneath the numbers.

Some advisors even avoid deeper conversations, assuming the plan will do the work for them. They offer explanation instead of rapport, strategy instead of sincerity. And then they're surprised when the prospect doesn't move forward. A plan only starts to matter once trust is in place. Without it, even the best advice can fall flat. With it, the same plan becomes a lever, something the client can actually use.

Trust breakers: how good advisors sabotage themselves

Most advisors don't mean to erode trust. But that doesn't stop it from happening. It's often not what they say. It's how they carry themselves. One of the biggest trust-breakers? Talking too much. In recorded discovery sessions, advisors often dominated the conversation, sometimes speaking seven times more than the prospect. When you talk more than you listen, you (obviously) fill airtime. Moreover, you send a signal: your agenda matters more than theirs.

Another trust-breaker is assuming instead of asking. Many advisors leap into solution mode before they fully understand what's on the prospect's mind. They diagnose without listening. They offer a roadmap without knowing the destination.

Then there are the quiet missteps, easy to miss, but loud in their impact. Prospects notice when you're late. When you reschedule too often. When you interrupt. When you forget what they shared. One of the most damaging missteps? A glance at your phone, what psychologists call "phubbing." Even that split-second check can leave someone feeling dismissed, disrespected, and disconnected. Research shows that even having a phone visible during a face-to-face interaction, without any use, erodes trust and closeness. And in moments when emotional safety is still forming, that glance can undo everything. If trust is a bridge, these behaviors are the cracks in its foundation.

Trust builders: the behaviors that prospects respond to

Trust builds through your way of being with people: your focus, your curiosity, your steadiness. Through small, intentional behaviors that make your sincerity as clear as your skill. It starts with real listening, not the kind that waits to speak, but the kind that reflects, pauses, and responds with care. It grows with real curiosity. Not about the portfolio. About the person. What they fear. What they value. It deepens when you slow down, name what matters, and create space for honesty. And sometimes, it's built with one sentence.

One of the most overlooked moments in a discovery meeting is the opportunity to say, clearly and explicitly, that everything shared is confidential.

It might feel obvious to you, but don't assume the prospect knows that, especially if they're about to share something personal. Say it directly: "Everything we talk about today is confidential. Nothing leaves this room without your permission." If you're a CFP® or a fiduciary, you can go still further. For example: "As a CFP®, it's part of my Code of Ethics to maintain confidentiality and protect the privacy of client information."

In smaller communities, that assurance is even more powerful. When everyone knows everyone, privacy is sacred. The most trusted advisors won't even mention a prospect's name without permission. As one advisor put it: In our town, people know who you're working with, unless they're working with me.

Trust is also built through follow-through, when you say you'll follow up, and you do. When you show up on time. When you answer hard questions clearly and without hedging. And finally, trust is built through vulnerability. Prospects don't expect you to know everything. But they do expect you to be honest. If you don't know, say so. If something's uncertain, say so. Vulnerability builds credibility faster than polish ever will.

Practicing trust: how habits reinforce connection

Trust builds over time, through attention, consistency, and small moments that add up. It doesn't arrive all at once. It's something you do, again and again, until it becomes part of how you work. Many advisors talk too much not because they're self-centered, but because silence feels uncomfortable. Because they think trust must be earned through expertise. Or because they're caught in a habit loop: cue, talk, reward. But the brain is trainable, and trust-building behaviors can become habits.

Pause before you respond. Speak in short, intentional bursts. Reflect what you heard before you advise. Meet them with your full focus and none of your agenda. The more you do this, the more natural it becomes. Eventually, it forms a rhythm your prospects feel. They feel safe. They open up. They trust you.

The trust advantage: why this matters more than ever

In today's advisory world, technical skill is assumed. Prospects expect it. They can research your services, read your blog, compare your fees. What they can't get from a website is how they feel sitting across from you.

That first exhale, the moment something real is said and genuinely received. That's when trust takes root. If your prospect walks out and tells a friend, "I don't know what it was. I simply felt like I could trust them," you've done what matters most.

Thoughts to carry forward

1. Prospects decide to trust based on how they feel, not what they're told.
2. Small behaviors shape that emotional trust: focused listening, full attention, reliability.
3. Trust is built through habits, not performances.

8

DECISION FATIGUE AND COGNITIVE LOAD

Helping prospects navigate overwhelm

The mental overload problem

Discovery can be disorienting. New terms, unfamiliar ideas, sizing up the advisor. And all at once. Advisors, eager to impress, often share too much too fast. Research shows that when people are overwhelmed, their ability to engage drops sharply. Instead of building confidence, overload halts momentum. In that first meeting, a prospect's ability to process and engage is fragile. If mental strain runs too high, the relationship can end before it begins.

Why overwhelm stalls decision-making

The brain is built for efficiency. Faced with financial complexity, it takes shortcuts; delaying action, sticking to the status quo, or opting out completely. What matters most isn't the volume of information, but the way it's structured, paced, and delivered to support understanding.

It's easy to misread decision fatigue as fear or inertia, but they arise from different roots. Fear drives avoidance to protect emotionally, while fatigue stems from cognitive depletion. Either way, the result is the same: no forward motion. But the solution is different. When fatigue sets in, don't push, simplify. Fatigue doesn't call for pressure. It calls for cognitive ease.

Understanding cognitive load

Every conversation with a prospect demands their attention, but attention isn't free. It draws on something psychologists call *cognitive load*, the total mental effort required to process information. When that load gets too heavy, people stop absorbing. They nod, they smile, but they're gone.

Cognitive load comes in three forms. First, there's *intrinsic load*, which is tied to the content itself. Some ideas are, by their nature, complex. Retirement income planning, for instance, or the difference between term and whole life insurance. That's not something you can always simplify, but it helps to name it and pace it appropriately.

Then there's *extraneous load*, the unnecessary strain we create through poor communication. Jargon, cluttered slides, inconsistent explanations, even a distracting environment. All of these pull mental energy away from the core idea.

Finally, there's *germane load*, which is the good kind. This is the mental effort it takes to organize new information, connect it to existing knowledge, and make sense of it. It's what learning actually feels like when it's working.

Your job as an advisor is to manage all three. That means simplifying where you can, eliminating distractions where you must, and focusing the conversation on what matters most to this person, in this moment. Clean up the visuals. Cut the tangents. Replace the jargon with real language tied to real life. Make the path as clear as possible so the prospect can walk it without stumbling, and still have enough energy left to want to keep going.

Reducing friction in the first conversation

Early meetings are high-stakes moments. Prospects arrive with their guard up, not because they're skeptical of your expertise, but because financial decisions are inherently vulnerable. What they're sizing up, often without realizing it, isn't your knowledge alone, but how you make them feel. Before they assess your competence, they're scanning for safety. Emotional cues like tone, posture, presence, and pacing carry more weight than charts or credentials. Warmth isn't fluff. It's a fast-track to trust. And trust is what makes people receptive. Receptivity, in turn, creates momentum.

This is where many advisors unintentionally create friction. In the rush to demonstrate value, they overexplain. They lean on technical depth before building emotional context. They offer a buffet of investment paths, thinking choice is power, when in fact, too much choice feels like pressure. Behavioral finance is clear on this: an overload of options doesn't empower, it paralyzes.

The goal of the first conversation isn't mastery. It's orientation. It's helping the prospect feel grounded, in control, and seen. That requires simplicity, not simplification. It means listening more than you explain. Telling stories instead of showing charts. Connecting ideas to their actual life instead of abstract theory. What lasts is what lands emotionally. When the conversation starts with safety and clarity, you earn the right to go deeper. Without that grounding, even the best advice won't land.

Clear ground before commitment

Discovery works best when it clears the air. When mental clutter is reduced, better questions emerge, thinking becomes steadier, and alignment feels possible. Decisions come more easily when the path ahead feels less fogged in. That's why the goal early on isn't to rush toward recommendations. It's to create clarity.

This starts by narrowing the conversation to one core issue that matters most. Rather than overwhelming prospects with abstract data, bring the discussion to life with real-world stories they can relate to. And most importantly, guide gently. Focus first, decide later.

Structuring a discovery meeting that works

When a conversation is well-structured, prospects leave feeling lighter, not more confused. You might try this approach to ease cognitive strain without sacrificing depth:

- **Start by building warmth:** Ask open-ended, personal questions. Share a story or two that humanizes the experience and sets the tone for real connection.
- **Uncover what matters most:** Try: "What's your biggest financial concern right now?" Then listen. Don't interrupt. Reflect their words back to them so they feel heard.
- **Offer a clear, gentle next step:** Recap what you've heard. Suggest a follow-up that feels helpful, not urgent.

Overload often shows up as hesitation: repeated questions, long pauses, or requests for time. But with the right rhythm, those signals become rare.

Be the simplifier, not the persuader

The advisors who lead most effectively are those who prioritize simplicity over complexity. By simplifying decisions and reducing mental strain, they create a process that feels natural, empowering, and human. In a noisy, complex industry, the advisor who offers a clear path forward wins.

Thoughts to carry forward

1. Prospects entering discovery meetings are often mentally overloaded, and excess information or complexity leads to decision fatigue rather than engagement.
2. Advisors who simplify their message, minimize cognitive load, and prioritize emotional connection build comprehension, confidence, and movement.
3. The most effective meetings are structured around warmth, listening, and a sense of ease, not technical depth or early persuasion.

9

NAVIGATING DIFFICULT PROSPECT EMOTIONS

Turning Tension Into Opportunity

Meeting emotion with skill, not fear

You can't plan for the moment someone shares the thing they've been carrying for years. But you can be ready for it. That's emotional skill. And it matters more than any spreadsheet.

Research shows that emotions are present during roughly 90% of our waking moments. We're feeling something almost all the time. Most emotions stay below the surface, unnoticed, yet they quietly shape how we interpret information, perceive risk, and make decisions. And this emotional backdrop has consequences. In a prospect meeting, that emotional undercurrent can mean the difference between engagement and resistance. And yet, only a third of people can accurately name what they're feeling in the moment.

That's why emotional intelligence matters. Advisors who notice subtle cues don't try to fix or diagnose. They simply meet people where they actually are.

Recognizing and responding to emotional triggers

Uncomfortable emotions don't always arrive with recognizable shape. They often appear through a stray comment, a sudden pause, or a shift in tone or posture. Some prospects name past financial traumas such as loss, bankruptcy, or betrayal. Others allude to fears like running out of money, disappointing family, or losing control.

These moments require more than surface listening. Pay close attention to non-verbal cues: tension in the jaw, avoidance of eye contact, hesitation. The deeper emotion usually shows up between the words.

Understanding the impact of financial trauma

Trauma leaves its mark on more than memory. It imprints itself on financial behavior. Someone who experienced financial insecurity as a child might be overly cautious or anxious. A person burned by investment fraud may fear even reasonable risk.

Consider Miguel. After losing substantial savings in a business partnership gone wrong, he stopped trusting financial professionals altogether. He held excessive cash, avoiding investments that could grow his wealth. Only when his advisor acknowledged Miguel's fears, without pressure, did he begin to rebuild trust and make healthier decisions.

Or Sofia, who watched her parents struggle in retirement. The experience left her terrified to spend any of her own savings. Her advisor validated that fear, then proposed tiny, low-risk steps. Over time, Sofia's anxiety eased, and her confidence grew.

The advisor's emotional toolkit

Guiding prospects through emotional terrain takes more than technical expertise. It requires a mindset, a kind of emotional toolkit that helps the advisor stay present, responsive, and clear. Empathy allows them to understand without absorbing. Active listening creates space for truth to emerge. Validation affirms emotional reality, even when not every belief needs to be endorsed. And emotional resilience helps the advisor remain steady while supporting others through difficult conversations. Of equal importance is knowing your boundaries. Care deeply, but do not carry the weight alone.

A five-step method for navigating sensitive conversations

When tough emotions arise, slow down. The financial agenda can wait. Here's a practical framework to guide your next conversation:

1. **Pause and Acknowledge:** "I notice this topic brings up strong feelings. Do you feel comfortable talking about this?"
2. **Create Safety:** "This is a confidential space, and there's no judgment here."
3. **Listen Deeply:** Let silence do some of the talking. Don't rush to fix. Give them your full attention. Nothing else.
4. **Reflect and Validate:** "I hear that you're worried about repeating past mistakes. That makes complete sense, given what you've been through."
5. **Collaboratively Explore:** "Knowing how this impacted you, what would feel like a safe next step?"

An example:

Prospect: "I lost everything in the market once. The idea of investing again terrifies me."

Advisor: "I can see how much that past loss still affects you. It's understandable you'd feel cautious."

Prospect: "It's always in the back of my mind. I never want to feel that helpless again."

Advisor: "Of course. What would need to be different for you to feel safe moving forward?"

Common mistakes advisors make, and how to avoid them

Even well-meaning advisors can mishandle emotional conversations, often without realizing it. One common misstep is jumping too quickly to solutions. When someone is vulnerable, they're looking for more than answers. They are looking to feel seen. They want to be recognized as much as they want things resolved. Another pitfall is minimizing emotion. Phrases like, "Don't worry, it'll all work out," may be meant to soothe, but often come across as dismissive. A better response might sound like, "Given your past, your concern makes complete sense."

Advisors may also take a client's emotional response personally, interpreting anxiety or frustration as a sign they've failed to reassure. One advisor, Naomi, used to do exactly that. Over time, she learned to name the emotion without defensiveness: "This conversation stirred up strong feelings. Let's explore that together." With practice, emotional moments become less like threats to avoid and more like openings to lean into.

Emotional intelligence as a trust accelerator

Trust isn't built by solving problems quickly. It's built by seeing the person behind the problem. When advisors handle emotional complexity with care, they send a powerful message: *I see YOU first, and your investments second.* That kind of recognition is unforgettable, and it lays the groundwork for relationships that last.

The most effective advisors don't rush to reassure or fix. Instead, they pause. They listen for what's not being said. They acknowledge emotion without trying to mute it. In doing so, they turn tense or uncertain moments into something rare: a felt sense of empathy, honesty, and respect. These aren't optional niceties. They're trust accelerators. When used well, they deepen connection, expand possibility, and set the stage for meaningful, ongoing collaboration.

Thoughts to carry forward

1. Recognizing and validating prospect emotions builds trust and opens the door to deeper conversations.

2. Emotionally aware advisors pause before problem-solving and avoid language that dismisses prospect concerns.

3. Mastering emotional intelligence leads to stronger relationships, lasting loyalty, and greater fulfillment.

10
WHAT THEY'RE NOT SAYING

Reading the Subtle Clues

What they don't say speaks loudest

Perceptive financial advisors know that what a prospect isn't saying often matters more than what they are saying. A prospect might nod in agreement, respond politely, even make friendly conversation, yet something feels off. Their answers get vague. Their tone shifts. They laugh, nervously, at something important.

If you've ever walked away from a meeting sensing something was left unsaid, you're not alone. Prospects hold back for all kinds of reasons: fear, uncertainty, discomfort, or simply not knowing how to say what they're really thinking. And when they do withhold something, it's rarely obvious. But the signs are there, if you're paying close attention.

Noticing what's left unsaid

In an ideal world, every prospect would arrive ready to open up about their hopes, fears, and financial concerns. In reality, many show up guarded. Some are afraid of being judged, worried they'll be told they've made years of wrong decisions. Others feel intimidated by the process itself, unsure what's expected. Then there are those who think they're being transparent but haven't yet admitted the real concern even to themselves.

Recognizing this requires more than listening. It means reading between the lines, noticing tone, body language, and those brief hesitations that suggest something deeper. Nonverbal behavior is often the first clue. A prospect who keeps their arms crossed might not be entirely comfortable, even if they're polite. A lack of eye contact, sudden fidgeting, or a subtle shift in posture, these are small but telling.

Then there's how they speak. Someone who usually answers with confidence might hedge. Instead of "Yes, I'm confident in our retirement plan," they say, "I think we're okay." They use qualifiers, "I guess," "I suppose," that leave room for doubt.

Sometimes, the hesitation is in the silence. A brief pause before answering, hinting at a struggle beneath the surface. Or a quick subject change. Or a joke. These moments may be brief, but once you start seeing them, you'll notice them everywhere. Prospects won't always say what they're thinking.

But they're always evaluating. Their words may be warm. Their tone may be polite. But their body language might tell a different story.

This is where warmth matters most. It shows up in your words, and in what you notice. If they feel genuinely acknowledged, not assessed, they start to relax. Subtle signs of unease are easier to miss when you're focused on sounding competent. It's not polish that earns trust. It's how tuned in you are. And it starts with what you notice. As we've explored, prospects instinctively assess whether you're trustworthy and capable. When they feel unsure, about you, the process, or themselves, that balance falters. And their cues change. Spotting those shifts takes patience. You're not looking to fix or push. You're looking to notice what might be going unsaid.

When to gently push, and when to step back

Once you sense a prospect is holding something back, it can be tempting to press. Sometimes, that's the right move. A gentle question like, "Can you tell me more about that?" can open the door. But if you press too soon, they might shut down. The key is knowing the difference.

Some prospects hesitate at first but stay engaged. They pause before responding, then lean in and share thoughtful answers. In those moments, a bit of encouragement, such as "That's interesting. Can you elaborate?" can help them continue.

Other times, you feel them pulling back. Their body language closes off. Their responses shrink. Their discomfort grows. Push here, and you'll lose them. It's better to acknowledge the tension and give them space. Saying, "I know this can be a tough thing to think about. There's no rush," reassures them. Switching topics, for now, can help them relax, so you can revisit the issue later. Not every pause needs to be explored. But each one holds a clue, if you're listening closely.

The art of responding without making prospects defensive

Nothing shuts down a conversation faster than making someone feel interrogated. It happens easily. Rapid-fire questions can leave a prospect feeling scrutinized. Because the way you ask shapes the meaning of the question itself.

A question like, "Why haven't you done more to prepare for retirement?" almost always triggers defensiveness. But "When you think about retirement, what's your biggest concern?" invites dialogue. The question matters, but your response to the answer is what leaves the mark.

If someone shares a fear, like running out of money or a past mistake, the worst move is to jump straight into solutions. Start by acknowledging: "That makes a lot of sense," or "I can understand why that would be on your mind." These short phrases validate emotion. Only then should you pivot to advice. Make them feel heard before you make them feel advised.

The power of patience

Some prospects open up right away. Others need time. Honesty takes time. It grows, moment by moment, each time the other person feels safe enough to speak freely. By noticing the subtle cues, knowing when to press and when to pause, and responding with empathy instead of urgency, you create the space for real conversations, ones that go beyond the numbers, into the reasons they came to you in the first place.

Thoughts to carry forward

1. Prospects often hold back in discovery meetings. Their hesitation shows up in subtle ways, vague answers, deflections, shifts in body language.
2. The key to breakthrough moments is knowing when to gently invite deeper sharing, and when to give space.
3. When you observe carefully, lead with warmth, and respond with empathy, you build the trust that opens the door to the conversations that matter most.

11

LOSS AVERSION AND THE FEAR OF CHANGE

Understanding What Really Drives Decisions

The tension behind prospect resistance

Prospects don't freeze from indifference. They freeze because change feels risky. Even when it's rational. What they're afraid of isn't just making the wrong decision. It's living with the regret. That's the power of loss aversion: it keeps people stuck in situations they know aren't working, simply because the alternative feels scarier.

Financial advisors often meet prospects who know they need to make a change but hesitate. They see the problems, value the advice, but still delay the decision. This hesitation is rarely due to a lack of understanding. It's often rooted in psychology.

People naturally avoid loss more than they pursue gain. Even when staying put carries financial risks, the emotional pull of avoiding regret often outweighs logical reasoning. Understanding this reluctance is critical. Effective conversations help prospects feel grounded and ready to move. Logic alone rarely gets them there.

Loss aversion, inertia, and the comfort of the familiar

Prospects resist switching advisors, adjusting their strategies, or making decisions. Not because they're unaware, but because change feels like potential loss. Status quo bias amplifies this instinct. Inaction feels safer.

For example, a prospect may know they're paying high fees for underperformance but still hesitate. A new advisor could be worse. The uncertainty of change feels more threatening than the known frustration they're living with. That's why change must be framed as improvement, not disruption. Don't focus only on the cost of staying. Spotlight what's possible if they move.

The fear of the unknown

Uncertainty has a powerful influence on decision-making. It's not always driven by how much someone knows. More often, it stems from what the decision represents. Even simple choices can take on unexpected weight when they stir questions about identity, control, or the possibility of future regret.

Take the example of a prospect who has managed their own portfolio for years. They know they could benefit from professional guidance, but quiet fears creep in. *What if I lose control? What if I don't understand the changes? What if I end up worse off?* These aren't rational calculations. They're emotional reflexes.

To ease that fear, advisors can offer a clear roadmap that outlines what to expect. They can start small, such as suggesting a portfolio review instead of proposing full engagement upfront. And they can share real stories of others who hesitated, then found confidence in the process. Small steps feel manageable. All-or-nothing decisions rarely do.

The weight of past choices

Sometimes the obstacle isn't the future. It's the past. Prospects often justify old decisions to avoid feeling like they made a mistake. This is the sunk cost fallacy: sticking with something simply because they've already invested time, money, or loyalty.

A prospect may resist selling an underperforming stock because selling confirms a loss. Or they may hold on to an advisor who no longer fits. Out of loyalty, not alignment. To help prospects move forward, normalize the pivot.

An advisor might say:

> *"Good decisions aren't about never changing course. They're about adapting as life evolves."*

> *"The best investors know when something no longer fits and adjust accordingly."*

Change isn't an indictment of the past. It's a commitment to the future.

Creating clarity and confidence in discovery meetings

Discovery meetings quietly set the tone for how change is approached and whether it feels possible. When prospects feel emotionally and cognitively grounded, they're far more open to considering new possibilities. That grounding doesn't happen by accident. It's built through a few key practices.

First, eliminate ambiguity from the start. Uncertainty creates resistance, even if it's subtle. By clearly setting expectations, what the meeting is, what it isn't, you help the prospect relax into the conversation. A simple statement like, "Today, our focus is, above all else, to understand where you are and what's on your mind. There's no pressure to make any decisions," does more than clarify logistics. It creates calm by establishing boundaries.

Second, make change feel manageable. Big decisions often trigger fear, but small, reversible steps feel safer. Rather than asking for commitment upfront, ease into it. Offer a side-by-side comparison, suggest a limited review project, or provide a planning roadmap with no obligation to implement. Each of these soft approaches reduces perceived risk and builds confidence in the process.

Finally, be mindful of framing. While it's tempting to highlight potential losses to spur action, fear-based messages can backfire. People respond better to possibility than to pressure. Instead of saying, "If you don't change your plan, you could lose money," try, "By making a few small modifications, you'll give yourself more flexibility and peace of mind later." The goal is grounded optimism: inspire with what's possible, not fear of what might go wrong. Together, these small shifts help create an environment where prospects feel safe, seen, and ready to engage. And that's when meaningful change becomes possible.

Using stories to make change feel possible

Data explains. Stories shift people. When Krish and Myra Patel, both in their early sixties, met with their advisor, they were hesitant. They'd been with their previous advisor, a friend, for 20 years. But they were nearing retirement, and cracks had started to show: conservative investments, high fees, missed opportunities. Despite their concerns, they stalled.

Krish said, "We're comfortable with him. He's been with us for a long time. What if switching makes things worse?" Their advisor replied, "You don't have to make a big decision today. Let's take one small step. A side-by-side review. No pressure, only clarity."

That step was enough. Once they saw the comparison, the story changed. Within a month, they'd transitioned. A year later, Krish said, "I don't know why we waited so long. We feel more in control now." That's what progress looks like. Not pressure, but permission.

Making action feel like a choice

In your next discovery meeting, consider inviting the prospect into the conversation with a question like, "What concerns you most about staying in your current situation?" Follow that with a small, clearly defined next step, something that feels manageable, not overwhelming. You might also reframe a key point, shifting the focus from what they might lose to what they could gain.

Prospects don't need more pressure. They need a path that feels safe and clear. When the process feels collaborative and grounded in their priorities, action becomes more natural. Change begins to feel less like a risk and more like a decision they're ready to make.

Thoughts to carry forward

1. Many financial advisors unknowingly structure their discovery meetings like sales calls, which can trigger resistance from prospects.
2. The biggest obstacle advisors face isn't competition. It's prospect inertia. People resist change even when they recognize its benefits.
3. Instead of persuading, advisors should guide prospects to recognize their own need for change through thoughtful questions and by reframing the risks of inaction.

12

THE HIDDEN TRUTH

Why Prospects Don't Always Tell You Everything

When fear, not dishonesty, drives silence

Maria sat across from her advisor, Liam, smiling politely as he reviewed her retirement projections. She nodded when he spoke, answered when he asked, and kept her expression friendly, even when the topic turned to debt. "Nope, nothing major," she said, shifting slightly in her seat. Two months later, as Liam finalized her plan, he uncovered a critical detail: a second mortgage on a vacation home. Not only had Maria withheld it, but the payments were consuming nearly 40% of her income. Why didn't she mention it? Was it dishonesty? Or something else entirely?

Shame? Fear of judgment? The sense that it wasn't "relevant"? Liam assumed he'd asked the right questions. Maria assumed she had to filter her answers. Neither was fully wrong. But something important got lost in that gap.

Financial advisors encounter this scenario regularly; prospects who omit details, downplay financial stress, or avoid discussing certain topics. While it might be tempting to assume deception, the reality is far more psychological than intentional. The more advisors understand why prospects hesitate to be fully transparent, the better they can foster trust, uncover critical financial details, and help prospects move toward better decision-making.

Why prospects hold back

Money is more than the math. It's memory, identity, and emotion, often tangled with shame, fear, and regret. When prospects hold back in conversation, it's rarely because they're unwilling. More often, they're protecting something tender.

For many, the hesitation begins with fear of judgment. Even high earners can feel exposed when they admit to past missteps. A doctor making $400,000 a year might carry $100,000 in credit card debt. But disclosing that, even to a professional, can feel like admitting personal failure. Others worry that admitting gaps in savings or impulsive spending will make them seem irresponsible. These emotions run deep, and when prospects sense even a hint of condescension, they shut down.

Then there are those shaped by bad experiences. Some have worked with advisors who prioritized products over people, offering advice that felt more transactional than trustworthy. Others recall being dismissed or patronized when they tried to explain their financial concerns. For a widow pressured into a high-fee annuity she didn't understand, vulnerability in a new advisory relationship won't come easily.

And sometimes, the barrier is simple avoidance. Talking about money stirs anxiety, especially when there's debt, unfiled taxes, or patterns of emotional spending in the background. Avoidance becomes a form of self-protection. The thinking is: *If I don't bring it up, maybe it won't come up.* But silence doesn't equal peace. It's one important signal that trust hasn't yet been earned. Understanding these dynamics isn't about diagnosing your prospect—it's about meeting them with empathy. If you know why they're holding back, you're far better equipped to create a space they feel safe stepping into.

What silence hides

Most prospects aren't hiding the truth. Not intentionally. They're protecting themselves, from shame, judgment, and fear. In one study, 30% of clients admitted to withholding vital personal financial information from their advisor. Not prospects. Clients. Even in established relationships, that emotional caution persists. So imagine how much more guarded someone might be in a first meeting. The stakes feel higher, the exposure more acute, and the trust unproven. Recognizing this allows advisors to approach conversations with more empathy and less frustration.

How the brain responds to financial stress

When a prospect hesitates to open up, it's not always a matter of unwillingness. Often, it's neurological. The brain interprets financial stress much like physical danger, and that perception shapes behavior in powerful, often invisible ways.

The body's fight, flight, or freeze response shows up quickly when financial fear or shame enters the room. The fight, flight, or freeze response isn't limited to physical danger; it can also be triggered by financial fear or shame. When the brain perceives emotional threat, especially around money, the amygdala can take the lead, disrupting clear thinking. A prospect might become defensive ("That's not important right now"), try to move the conversation along too quickly ("I don't really want to get into that"), or go quiet, offering vague responses like ("I'm not sure, I'll have to check.") These behaviors aren't necessarily resistance. More often, they're a signal of mental overload. Even small cues, like avoiding eye contact or shifting in their seat, can point to a nervous system under strain.

The brain responds instantly, while neuroplasticity shapes its patterns over time. If someone grew up in a home where money triggered arguments, they may now feel anxious every time finances are discussed. If they were never taught the basics, admitting what they don't know can feel humiliating. Past mistakes, especially those that led to real consequences, can make even simple questions feel threatening. Financial transparency isn't only factual. It's foundational to feeling safe. It's about helping the brain shift from defense to openness, from survival mode to curiosity. And that shift doesn't happen with data. It happens with empathy, pacing, and presence.

Creating a climate for financial honesty

Honest conversations don't happen by default. They require an environment where people feel safe, emotionally, cognitively, and socially. When prospects sense judgment or pressure, they instinctively pull back. But when the space feels empathetic and non-threatening, they're far more likely to share the full picture.

One of the most effective ways to invite openness is to lead with warmth, and not with competence. While many advisors feel the need to establish their expertise upfront, connection often does more to move the conversation forward. Starting with a prompt like, "Tell me about your financial goals and what matters most to you," signals care before calculation. Even briefly sharing a personal financial lesson, something honest and human, can create instant rapport.

It also helps to normalize financial vulnerability. Many prospects feel like they're the only ones behind, the only ones carrying debt, or the only ones who don't understand the language of finance. That isolation makes honesty harder. Gently offering context, like how common it is to carry debt into retirement, or how many people struggle with budgeting, can diffuse shame. Phrases like, "A lot of people I work with have faced something similar," do more than reassure. They widen the lens.

And the questions you ask matter. Closed-ended questions tend to shut things down. Open, emotionally intelligent prompts create room for real dialogue. Instead of asking, "Do you have any debt?" try, "Are there any financial obligations that keep you up at night?" The difference isn't only in tone. It's the kind of answer it draws out. You'll often learn more by asking how a financial decision feels than by focusing on the numbers alone.

Honesty tends to surface when people feel seen, not sized up. The more grounded and attentive the environment, the more likely prospects are to name the challenges that actually need addressing.

The truth comes with trust

Honest conversations take root in the right conditions. When prospects feel safe, genuinely heard, and free to be real, something deeper starts to unfold. Safety is earned, not assumed. Empathy works better than interrogation, and the right environment unlocks real transparency. When advisors create space for honest dialogue, prospects begin to open. Offering the full picture: the numbers, and the hopes and fears they carry. And that's when true financial planning begins.

Thoughts to carry forward

1. Prospects often withhold financial details due to shame, fear of judgment, or past negative experiences, not deception.
2. Financial stress triggers avoidance behaviors, making it essential for advisors to recognize emotional cues and respond with empathy.
3. Creating a safe, judgment-free space through warmth, normalization, and open-ended questions encourages prospects to share the full picture.

PART THREE

Designing a Trust-Centered Discovery Meeting

You've seen your own patterns. You've started to understand what's happening emotionally for your prospect. Now comes the turning point: how do you lead a discovery conversation that earns real trust? Not through charm or control, but through intention, presence, and a structure that invites openness. This section gives you the tools to flip the old dynamic. You'll learn how to slow the conversation down, ask better questions, and build trust without ever needing to "sell."

Chapters in this section

- **Flipping the Script:** Reversing the Old Discovery Dynamics
- **Competence vs. Connection:** What Prospects Are Actually Testing
- **The Flat Table:** Reimagining Power in Discovery
- **Using Personal Stories:** How to Build Deeper Emotional Trust
- **The Art of Asking Thought-Provoking Questions:** Inviting Prospects Into Reflection
- **Demonstrating True Competence:** Leading Without Dominating
- **The Fee Conversation:** When and How to Discuss Pricing with Confidence
- **Tech Without the Talk:** Using Tools Without Losing Touch
- **Leading Discovery in a Digital World:** Staying Human Across Any Format

Designing a Trust-Centered Discovery Meeting

13
FLIPPING THE SCRIPT

Reversing the Old Discovery Dynamics

Turning discovery into your greatest differentiator

For many advisors, a discovery meeting serves as an evaluation: a chance to gather facts, assess assets, and decide whether a prospect is worth pursuing. The mindset runs so deep that most never stop to question it. But what if that entire approach is backward?

Most discovery meetings are designed to extract information, not deliver value. Advisors come in with an agenda: gather financial details, assess fit, and decide next steps. But from the prospect's perspective, this often feels transactional. Like a box-checking exercise, not a meaningful conversation. Now, imagine shifting that dynamic.

What if, instead of focusing on your process, you made discovery about the prospect's experience? What if every prospect left their first meeting feeling heard, understood, and empowered, whether they hired you or not? A great discovery meeting does more than gather data. It gives something back. Discernment, confidence, and control. This shift deepens trust, differentiates the advisor, and makes it far more likely that prospects will want to move forward.

Trust begins with partnership, not polish

Many advisors were trained to lead with answers, to demonstrate value quickly, to prove competence before trust is earned. But here's the tension: the more you try to impress, the less the prospect tends to share.

And yet, most advisors don't think of themselves as performing. They're being professional, sharing insights, explaining their process, offering reassurance. But even that can backfire when it makes the meeting about the advisor instead of the prospect. When the focus shifts to impressing, teaching, or leading too early, the prospect often pulls back.

In discovery meetings, over-explaining can become a way to maintain control, to steady yourself when the outcome feels uncertain. It's the subtle pressure to steer, to sound polished, to say the right things. But when the advisor does most of the talking, the prospect becomes an audience, not a participant. True discovery requires the opposite: a willingness to relinquish center stage. Not to withdraw, but to invite. To create the kind of space where people speak freely, not cautiously. That's not passivity. It's partnership in its most powerful form. When a discovery meeting becomes a stage, the conversation narrows. Prospects instinctively pull back. They give you merely enough to get through it, but not enough to build anything meaningful. Real trust doesn't come from presenting. It comes from how you're listening, not what you're saying.

A great question doesn't work alone. It needs space around it, the right conditions for thinking to happen. Skilled advisors rely less on clever phrasing or perfect timing, and more on presence. It's the quality of attention you offer, the silence you allow, the lack of judgment in your face or tone. It's the difference between a rapid-fire interview and a reflective pause. When prospects sense they're not being rushed, fixed, or sold, their defenses lower. They don't simply give better answers. They reach better thinking.

This is what gives discovery its distinct feel: more grounded, more secure. In a well-designed thinking environment, prospects don't feel like they're being evaluated, they feel like they're being understood. And the more they think out loud, the more they own what they're saying. That shift, from answering your questions to articulating their own truth, is what creates real insight. It's not the question alone that creates value. It's the space it opens up.

Discovery changes when you show up as a partner. Not to dazzle or convince, but to stand with the other person in what matters to them. To flatten the dynamic. To let go of the pedestal. You're not the only expert. They're the expert on their life. On their fears, regrets, hopes, and doubts. Your role is to uncover, not convince. To explore, not explain.

Here's how that shift sounds in practice:

Instead of: "Let me walk you through our process,"

Try: "Would it be okay if I asked a few questions to understand what matters most to you?"

Instead of: "Here's how we help clients like you,"

Try: "What would make this relationship feel valuable to you?"

Clarity over complexity

Many prospects come into a discovery meeting carrying more than the numbers. They bring vague financial worries, unspoken goals, and often, quiet fears about the future. Some have only ever experienced transactional conversations with financial professionals. Others have avoided financial discussions altogether.

A well-run discovery meeting offers something different, something many have never encountered before. It creates space to articulate what truly matters, without judgment or pressure. Through thoughtful guidance, advisors can help prospects untangle their concerns, clarify their priorities, and begin to see a path forward. The goal isn't to rush into solutions. It's to create clarity, reduce anxiety, and help them leave the meeting feeling lighter and more confident.

Helping prospects think clearly

One of the advisor's most overlooked strengths in discovery is the ability to ask questions that create space. These moments give prospects room to slow down, reflect, and reach insights that matter to them. Good questions do more than gather facts. They help people make sense of what they're feeling and clarify what they truly want.

A well-placed question can reframe the conversation: "What would have to be true for you to feel financially secure?" A thoughtful prompt could bring focus: "If you had to choose between retiring early and leaving a financial legacy, which feels more important?" And sometimes, a small observation sparks recognition: "You've mentioned freedom several times today. Would you say that's a core value for you?" When prospects name their own insights, they begin to take real ownership of their decisions. That sense of clarity and agency makes them far more likely to engage fully in the advisor's process.

The advisor's secret weapon: paraphrasing

Paraphrasing may be one of the most underappreciated tools in an advisor's discovery process. Many prospects struggle to articulate their financial goals, let alone the deeper aspirations behind them. When an advisor listens closely and restates what they've heard with care and clarity, something shifts. The prospect hears their own thoughts reflected back, often more clearly than they could have expressed themselves, and that experience builds both confidence and trust.

This kind of paraphrasing does more than signal understanding. It helps shape direction. Sometimes people don't fully know what they want until they hear it framed back in simple, accurate terms. Phrases like "What I'm hearing is …" or "It sounds like your top priority is …" not only reassure the prospect that they've been heard but also invite them to refine their thinking. In that space, vague ideas can take on sharper definition, and real goals can begin to form.

Less persuasion, more presence

Many advisors enter discovery meetings with a subconscious urge to win: to prove themselves, to earn the yes. But what if that pressure is unnecessary? When an advisor views discovery as a valuable conversation, not a sales step, they naturally become more present and engaged. What sets you apart isn't always what you say. It's how deeply you listen. When prospects leave with more understanding than they arrived with, that's the mark of a meaningful conversation.

Finding your balance: the Goldilocks principle

When advisors begin rethinking discovery, a common question surfaces: How much structure is too much? If the meeting is too loose, it drifts. If it's too rigid, it starts to feel like an interview. The most effective advisors find a middle ground, one that offers enough clarity to stay focused, but enough flexibility to stay human.

On one end of the spectrum is what might be called the Interrogation. This is the checklist-style meeting, where the advisor leads with a string of fact-finding questions: "What's your income?" "Do you have a will?" "What's your current asset allocation?" These are necessary questions, but when they come too early, the conversation can feel sterile, more like filling out a form than building a relationship.

On the other end is the Coffee Date. These meetings are warm and conversational, full of rapport but lacking direction. There's no clear framework, and no real momentum. The prospect might leave thinking, "That was nice," but not necessarily, "That was helpful."

Then there's the Goldilocks approach, the balance point. Here, the advisor creates both safety and structure. They ask thoughtful, open-ended questions, while also keeping the conversation on course. There's room for the discussion to breathe, but also a sense of purpose guiding it forward. Great discovery doesn't feel scripted, but it doesn't meander either. It feels like a meaningful conversation with a clear destination, led by someone who knows how to get there.

Turning insight into action

A well-run discovery meeting uncovers important details and also helps the prospect feel heard, understood, and more confident about what comes next. One way to reinforce that impact is to adopt a simple rhythm at the close of every conversation.

Begin by summarizing what you've heard. Reflect back the key themes, concerns, and goals the prospect shared. Summarizing what you've heard reinforces that you were listening and also gives the prospect a clearer view of their own story. That reflection alone can shift how someone sees their financial picture.

Next, invite refinement. Use prompts like, "Does this sound right to you?" or "Is there anything you'd add or change?" These small questions hand agency back to the prospect and signal that this is a collaborative process, not a one-sided presentation.

Then, reframe goals in a way that feels affirming and aspirational. Instead of saying, "You don't want to run out of money in retirement," try, "You want the freedom to enjoy retirement on your terms, with financial security that lasts." The goal is to move the conversation from fear to possibility.

Finally, close with a clear, manageable next step. Something like, "Based on today's conversation, I'll draft a strategy that reflects your top priorities. We'll review it together next time," gives structure without pressure and reinforces progress.

Mastering this rhythm, summarizing, confirming, reframing, and clarifying, can transform a routine meeting into a meaningful turning point. It signals that you're guiding the conversation. Listening with direction, shaping the conversation into something useful.

Be different

A discovery meeting should never feel like an interview. It should feel like the first, most important conversation a prospect has ever had about their financial future. When you create value in real time, you remove the need for persuasion. The prospect leaves clearer, more confident, and ready to act, with you as their trusted guide.

The traditional approach is rooted in fact-finding. A prospect-first approach shifts the focus to trust-building, ensuring that every interaction is meaningful, even if the relationship doesn't move forward. By prioritizing presence, listening, and meaningful conversation over sales pressure, advisors transform discovery from a process to an experience. One that prospects appreciate, remember, and are far more likely to say yes to.

Thoughts to carry forward

1. Discovery reveals what matters most to the prospect. It's a conversation that reaches beneath the surface, to what matters most.
2. Forget the scripted lines and deepen the relationship by listening hard, asking sharper questions, and reflecting back with precision.
3. The right balance of structure and spontaneity turns a meeting into a moment that sticks.

14

COMPETENCE
VS. CONNECTION

What Prospects Are Actually Assessing

The mid-air shift in strategy

Hannah, a midcareer advisor, took pride in her market knowledge. Being prepared meant proving she knew her stuff, so she opened discovery meetings with charts and projections, a confident show of competence. At one initial meeting, she launched into her usual rhythm until she noticed the couple across from her staring blankly. They weren't disagreeing. They were disengaging. She pressed on, but their posture said the real conversation was happening silently: *This isn't about us.*

When she finally paused, the husband spoke about his father's uncertain retirement. The wife voiced worries about college costs. Numbers weren't their first language. Fear was. Hannah closed her laptop and leaned forward. "Help me understand what retirement security means to you."

The air shifted. Shoulders dropped. They spoke of mornings on a porch, routines they loved, schools for their kids. Hannah listened more than she spoke. When she did speak, she bridged her expertise to the life they described, not the other way around. She hadn't led with performance. She hadn't needed to. Competence mattered, but connection opened the door.

The science of trust: warmth before competence

Research backs up Hannah's pivot. Social psychologist Amy Cuddy and colleagues found that in new encounters we instinctively assess warmth, trustworthiness, friendliness, sincerity, before competence. These two traits account for about 80% of how we judge others, with warmth leading.

Evolution may explain why. For early humans, knowing intentions mattered more than knowing skills. Only after feeling safe did abilities matter. A *Trends in Cognitive Sciences* study confirmed the pattern: in short interactions, people judged trustworthiness before intelligence or capability.

For advisors, the implication is blunt. Technical skill alone won't win trust. Clients must feel respected, heard, and emotionally safe before they can absorb expertise. In a world where information is easy to find, what's scarce is an advisor who can guide people through emotionally charged decisions with clarity, empathy, and steadiness. Ironically, starting with warmth often makes you seem more competent, because listening and curiosity are interpreted as signs of control and mastery.

Where advisors go wrong

Many advisors default to competence in ways that replace connection. In Discovery Lab recordings, some spoke up to seven times more than the prospect, turning the meeting into a one-way broadcast. In a 60-minute session, that leaves the prospect speaking for only eight minutes, hardly enough to feel heard.

Others front-load credentials, listing degrees and designations before building rapport. Without a foundation of connection, these facts can feel like a barrier, not a bridge. Another misstep is skipping the emotional layer. Advisors who jump straight to facts miss the chance to surface fears, hopes, and motivations, the drivers behind decisions. Clients may nod along but disengage, withholding information critical to good advice. When connection is missing, even accurate, well-reasoned guidance can land flat or be ignored.

Exceptions that prove the principle

There are moments when competence must lead. In crises, a pending loan default, sudden inheritance, or market crash, clients need decisive action. Warmth alone won't solve the problem, though even here, a brief word of reassurance can steady the room. Highly analytical prospects such as engineers, attorneys, or executives may also respond best to logic first. With them, evidence or a model can be the right opening, as long as you still signal early that you see the human stakes beneath the data.

How to shift your approach

Advisors can build trust faster by adjusting three habits:

- **Lead with curiosity, not credentials:** Ask open-ended questions like, "What's important to you about this decision?" Listen without rushing to fill the silence.
- **Validate before solving:** Acknowledge the emotion before addressing the problem: "I can see why that's weighing on you."
- **Show understanding before showing expertise:** Reflect back what you've heard, such as "Your biggest worry is outliving your savings," before explaining your plan.

Small habits amplify these behaviors: pausing two seconds after a client finishes speaking, mirroring their phrasing when restating concerns, and starting each meeting with a personal question unrelated to finance.

Lead with connection, follow with competence

Hannah's instinct to lead with expertise was common, especially early in her career. But her pivot reflected a deeper truth: people think more clearly when they're not bracing themselves. They can weigh more options and absorb more of your technical insight.

Competence may get you noticed. Connection keeps you trusted. Advisors who master one without the other risk mediocrity. Advisors who can do both, in the right order, become indispensable.

Thoughts to carry forward

1. Prospects instinctively assess warmth before competence, making connection the gateway to trust and the foundation for impactful advice.
2. Advisors undermine trust when they lead with expertise, overtalk, overload credentials, or skip the emotional layer.
3. Competence may lead in crises or with analytical clients but pairing it with warmth creates lasting influence.

15

THE FLAT TABLE

Reimagining Power in Discovery

What if you're not the expert in the room?

Here's the quiet truth: most discovery meetings begin with an unspoken hierarchy. You're the advisor. The one with the credentials, the track record, the answers. They're the prospect. The one with the questions, the uncertainty, the need.

That's the script we've been handed: be the expert, lead the meeting, prove your value quickly. But what if that model is holding you back? What if the most powerful move you can make isn't leading with answers, but creating space for theirs? Here's the irony: the harder you try to prove yourself, the quieter they get.

So let's ask a better question: what is the true role of an advisor in a discovery meeting? It's not to sell. It's not to persuade. It's not even to solve, not yet. It's to understand. And that requires partnership, not hierarchy.

The real expertise in the room

In this reimagined model, both people come to the table with essential expertise. The prospect is the expert on their own life, their goals, regrets, values, fears, and hopes. The advisor's strength isn't in delivering answers. It's in creating space for real thinking. Not by guiding the conversation, but by letting it unfold. This is the flat table. No pedestal. No power play. A shared space for mutual discovery. Nothing more, nothing forced.

Proof the table is flattening

This shift isn't abstract. It's already happening:

- 78% of consumers want to be actively involved in their financial planning.
- The CFP® Board defines planning as a collaborative process.
- 93% of highly collaborative advisors receive referrals, compared to 60% of their less collaborative peers.

Why old habits die hard, and what they cost

Many advisors were trained to equate expertise with control: say more, prove more, diagnose quickly, and speak with authority. Prospects today aren't chasing flash. They're drawn to real understanding. Meet them there, and they'll meet you with trust, and action. Still, many advisors fall back on habit, on proving themselves instead of connecting. Silence feels awkward. Not knowing feels vulnerable. Asking questions without preloaded answers feels risky.

But every time we lead with answers instead of curiosity, we shrink the discovery. We limit what the prospect is willing to share. And we risk missing the truth that could have changed everything. Hierarchy comforts the advisor. Partnership frees the prospect. Only one builds mutual respect.

Building trust through shared authorship

How do you flatten the table in practice? It starts with a shift in intention, from "Let me show you what I know" to "Help me understand what matters most to you." From "I have the answers" to "Let's figure this out together." This isn't passivity. It's a different kind of engagement. You're not pulling back. You're shifting the focus. And without the spotlight. Because asking great questions, listening generously, and following curiosity aren't soft skills. They're rare ones. And they signal something powerful: safety.

When a prospect senses you're not trying to control the conversation, they open up. When they feel their voice is shaping the process, trust begins. It's measured as much by your empathy as your expertise. That's shared authorship.

The role of humility, and the courage to not know

This is where many advisors feel the rub: "If I'm not offering insights, if I'm not adding value in real time, am I doing my job?" Yes, but it's a different job than you may be used to. You're not there to solve the problem in the first meeting. You're there to understand the problem behind the problem. Not to map the plan, but to understand what the plan needs to serve.

That takes humility. And it takes courage. Because when you let go of proving, you may feel exposed. You may wonder if you're doing enough. But when you make peace with not knowing, at least at first, you invite the prospect to bring their full self to the table. And when that happens, the real work begins.

What this looks like in practice

Imagine two advisors meeting the same prospect couple, John and Marisol, both nearing retirement. The first advisor, confident and polished, opens the meeting by thanking them for coming and immediately launching into his process. He walks them through a series of slides, highlights his credentials, and introduces his planning software. Then come the questions: "How much do you have in retirement accounts? What's your annual spending? Do you plan to work part-time after retirement?" He's professional and prepared. But he's clearly in the lead. John and Marisol answer politely, sticking to the facts. They provide the numbers he asks for but offer little else. The conversation stays surface-level.

The second advisor opens differently. She greets them warmly and sets a different tone from the outset. "I'm really glad you're here," she says. "Before we get into numbers or strategies, I want to understand what's going on in your life. What's making you curious, or maybe even a little uneasy, about the future?" She listens quietly. When they respond, she doesn't rush to fill the space. Instead, she follows up with gentle prompts. "Tell me more about that. How long have you been feeling this way? Why do you think this is coming up now?"

Eventually, Marisol leans in and says, "We're not only worried about running out of money. We're worried about making the wrong decisions and not being able to undo them." John adds, "Yeah. It's bigger than the finances. It's the next chapter. What do we do with all that time?" It's a quiet moment, but a defining one. Not because of anything the advisor said. But because of what the prospect felt safe enough to share.

Micro shifts that flatten the table

Flattening the table doesn't require grand gestures. Often, it's the micro shifts that make the biggest difference. It starts with language. Instead of saying, "Let me walk you through our process," try, "Would it be okay if I asked a few questions to better understand what matters most to you right now?" Rather than leading with, "Here's how we work with clients like you," ask, "What would make this relationship feel really valuable to you?" And before talking about the firm's services, consider starting with, "Can I first understand what a great outcome looks like for you?"

Your physical presence speaks as loudly as your words. Soften your posture. Avoid taking up too much space. Let your presence speak for you, calm, focused, and genuine. Use pauses with intention instead of filling every silence. Listen in a way that creates room for reflection. Listen with your eyes and ears, tuning in to words, energy, and movement alike.

And then there is pacing. Give your prospect time to think. Silence, when held with care, signals respect. Match their energy in a way that supports, not steers. Speak less. Ideally, your voice should carry no more than half the conversation, and often closer to a third. These small shifts can shift a meeting from transactional to collaborative. That's where discovery becomes real.

The long-term payoff of partnership

Some advisors wonder, "If I'm not leading with answers, how do I show my value?" The answer is simple, though not always easy. You show your value by creating a space where the client can show theirs. When someone feels truly listened to, you don't need to persuade. They start to believe in the process because they believe in you. With their money and with their story.

That kind of trust changes everything. It leads to clearer goals, because clients feel safe enough to be honest. It deepens engagement, because they're actively shaping the plan alongside you. And it builds lasting loyalty, because they know they're more than a file or a financial profile. They matter. In the long run, that's more than good business. It's meaningful work.

A note to the uneasy reader

If this all sounds counterintuitive, maybe even irresponsible, you're not alone. For many advisors, the idea of stepping back from the expert role feels like abandoning the very value they were trained to deliver. But before rejecting this outright, consider this: the old model of control and performance wasn't designed for today's client. It was built in an era when information was scarce and authority sold trust. That era is over. What clients need now isn't a performance. It's a partnership. The Flat Table isn't about doing less. It's about doing the harder work of listening first. And that kind of shift, while uncomfortable, opens doors to deeper trust, richer insight, and more lasting change.

Rediscovering your own curiosity

Here's the invitation: before your next discovery meeting, take a moment to pause. Let go of the urge to impress. Resist the default to lead with what you know. Instead, ask yourself a simple question: "What might I learn today that I couldn't possibly know unless they told me?" That question shifts everything. It opens the door to genuine curiosity, to a kind of listening that isn't about control, but about connection. That is the spirit of discovery. That is the heart of partnership. And that is what it means to sit at a flat table.

Thoughts to carry forward

1. Flatten the hierarchy: Ditch the expert pedestal. Discovery works when the conversation is real, not rehearsed.
2. Shift from answers to curiosity: understanding builds trust. Performance builds distance.
3. Practice shared authorship: Ask better questions, listen deeply.

16

USING PERSONAL STORIES

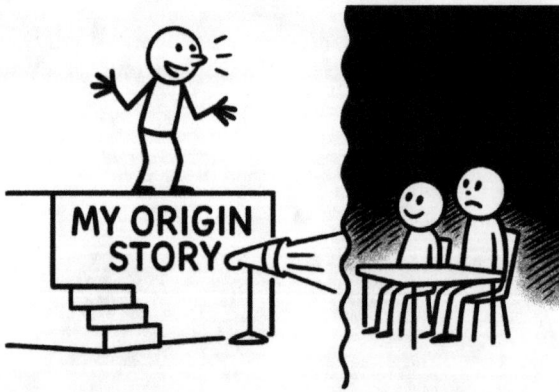

How to Build Deeper Emotional Trust

When to share your story, and why it matters

Good stories reveal something true. But very often in discovery, advisor stories reveal the wrong thing; misjudged timing, misplaced focus, or a need to impress. The truth is that humans are neurologically wired for story. Research shows that personal narratives trigger emotional resonance, foster empathy, and activate trust-based neural pathways. That's why a well-placed story, brief, relevant, and client-centered, can transform a moment of surface-level rapport into real relational depth.

In a discovery meeting, your story shouldn't shift the focus. It should open the door to theirs. A personal anecdote, especially your "why," signals authenticity, lowers emotional defenses, and invites clients to share what really matters to them.

Why personal stories matter in discovery

Behind every good story: a surge of dopamine, a spike in attention, a memory that sticks. Neuroscience shows that stories stimulate oxytocin (the "trust hormone") and engage the brain's empathy centers. That's why they're remembered, and why they matter.

Discovery meetings are rarely about spreadsheets alone. They're where emotion and identity come to the surface. A personal story, shared at the right moment, reminds the client they're speaking to a person, not only a technician. You're talking to someone who gets it. That kind of emotional resonance turns a transactional conversation into something far more powerful.

Sharing your "why," and how to do it well

One of the most effective ways to build early emotional engagement is to share why you do this work. Not as a pitch, but as a glimpse into what genuinely drives you.

For example:

> *"My father passed away unexpectedly without a financial plan. Watching my family struggle through that chaos shaped everything about the way I approach this work."*

It's not only what you know that stands out, but what genuinely matters to you. It makes your motivation tangible. And that sincerity is what earns a client's attention. But it only works when the story is clear, concise, and connected to what the client is feeling or facing. Otherwise, it lands as distraction, not connection.

Telling the right story, at the right time

Storytelling can be a powerful tool in discovery, but only when it's used with care. The right moment to share a personal anecdote is after the client has already opened up emotionally. Your story should echo what they've expressed, not steer the conversation somewhere new. If a client admits anxiety about market volatility, for example, a brief story about helping others navigate uncertainty can offer quiet reassurance. It normalizes fear, reinforces connection, and signals that they're not alone.

The key is intentional vulnerability. A little goes a long way. The purpose is to reveal something real enough to create resonance, while keeping the focus squarely on the client. Strong stories make space. Weak ones pull focus. If you're not sure which one you're telling, pause.

A well-placed story should be brief, about a minute or two, and directly connect to something the client has shared. And it should serve as a bridge back to them, not a detour. After you speak, leave space for the story to land. Then try asking, "How does that compare to what you've been thinking about?" That one question reframes the story as a mirror, something that reflects and deepens the client's own thinking.

Pitfalls to avoid

There are a few common pitfalls that can dull the impact of storytelling in a discovery conversation. Oversharing is one of them. A story that runs too long or becomes too emotionally charged can shift the dynamic, turning the client into an audience. Another misstep is using a story to shine the spotlight on yourself, especially if it's aimed at proving competence or showcasing success. And then there's timing. A story introduced too early, before real connection has been established, can feel out of place or forced.

A simple test can help. If you're telling the story because *you* need to say it, pause. If you're telling it because *they* need to hear it, you're likely in the right place to begin.

Practical storytelling cues

Effective storytelling depends as much on delivery as it does on content. Start by reading the room. Are they leaning in, nodding, making eye contact? Or are they pulling back, distracted, or disengaged? Let their body language guide your pacing. Match their tone, as well as their words. If they're speaking with intensity, meet that energy. If they're quiet or cautious, soften your approach.

Pay attention to how they connect. Some clients respond to emotion and personal detail. Others tune in more when the story is grounded in facts or strategy. The more you can alter your style to meet their way of processing, the more your story will land.

Examples in contrast

Consider a client who's navigating a career change. They express uncertainty and fear of the unknown. The advisor responds with a brief, sincere reflection: "That was a tough season when I went through something similar. What's this transition been like for you?" It's a short moment, but it does three things well. It acknowledges, relates, and then returns the focus to the client.

Now contrast that with an advisor who takes the same cue and responds with a five-minute story about launching their own firm and building it into a success. It may be impressive, but it misses the moment. The client is left wondering what any of it has to do with them.

Self-reflection for better storytelling

After a meeting, it's worth taking a moment to reflect on how your storytelling showed up. Did your story connect to the client's emotions or experience? Was it brief, clear, and sincere? Did it move the dialogue forward, or pull it off course? Most importantly, did it leave space for the client's voice?

The best stories don't dominate the conversation. They open it. A well-timed, well-told story does more than deliver information. It builds emotional credibility. It signals: *You can count on me. Not only with your money, but with your uncertainty too.* And that's when the real conversation begins.

Thoughts to carry forward

1. Storytelling works best when it's short, relevant, and client-centered.
2. Vulnerability earns trust only when it's used to create space, not take it.
3. Your story doesn't close the loop. It opens the door.

17

THE ART OF ASKING THOUGHT-PROVOKING QUESTIONS

Inviting Prospects Into Reflection

Why good questions aren't always good enough

Asking questions might feel like progress, but not all questions lead to insight. In our analysis of over 100 recorded discovery meetings, we found that 90+ percent of the questions asked were closed-ended. Prompts like, "Do you have a will?" or "Are you happy with your current advisor?" may check a box, but they rarely open a door. These kinds of questions gather data, not depth. For the prospect, it can feel less like a conversation and more like a checklist.

The best advisors take a different approach. They ask questions that slow things down and invite reflection. Instead of seeking a quick answer, they open space for the prospect to share the story behind the fact. Questions like, "What made you decide to create your will?" or "What's important to you in an advisory relationship?" signal that this is about understanding, not assessment.

These moments can't be rushed. They require presence, patience, and the willingness to sit with whatever comes up. That's where trust starts to build. Not in the facts alone, but in the feeling that someone is truly listening.

Asking questions that make prospects think

Not all questions are created equal, and not all conversations invite change. The kinds of questions you ask shape not only what you learn, but what the prospect learns about themselves. Closed-ended prompts tend to trigger quick replies: polished scripts, surface details, minimal reflection. But open-ended questions interrupt that rhythm. A prompt like "Tell me about …" invites a story. "What led you to …?" opens the door to memory, emotion, and deeper motivation.

When a prospect pauses before answering, that silence isn't resistance. It's a signal. They're thinking, maybe in a new way. And that's where real discovery begins. Skilled advisors make space for that pause. They follow threads gently, layering questions like "What else?" or "How did you come to feel that way?" often surfacing insights the prospect hadn't yet put into words. Framing matters, too. A question like "Are you worried about running out of money?" narrows the mind. "What would financial peace of mind look like for you?" opens it.

Neuroscience backs this up. Responding to open-ended questions activates broader and more complex brain networks than closed-ended ones. The prefrontal cortex, the brain's hub for decision-making, memory, and reasoning, lights up as prospects generate original thoughts. They're doing more than answering. They're making sense of things as they go. This effort creates cognitive engagement, which often feels like emotional engagement. What may look like a pause is actually mental scaffolding being built in real time. By contrast, closed-ended questions trigger recognition and recall, faster, easier, and far less revealing. Advisors who get this do more than ask smart questions. They shape spaces where better thinking can happen.

Why thinking matters in discovery

Thinking is where change begins. When a prospect is asked a question they haven't rehearsed, they share more than information. They begin to engage with their own thinking in a deeper way. They start connecting financial facts to personal values, past decisions to future possibilities. "I have a trust" becomes "I wanted my kids to have what I didn't."

These responses often go beyond surface-level answers. They mark a shift, moments where understanding deepens and something meaningful starts to take shape. When prospects reflect aloud, trust builds. They don't feel examined or judged. Reflection creates emotional safety, and emotional safety makes honesty possible.

And the more they think, the more it becomes theirs. Decisions anchored in personal insight tend to stick, because they're self-generated, not advisor imposed. Prospects leave with answers, and a sense of conviction. That's the shift discovery is designed to create.

The risk, and power, of "why"

"Why" can be illuminating, but it can also be provocative. A question like "Why haven't you saved more?" makes a prospect brace. It sounds like judgment, even if it isn't. The alternative is curiosity over critique. Asking "What has shaped your approach to saving over the years?" or "What led you to that decision?" lands as an invitation, not an interrogation. Used thoughtfully, "why" uncovers motivation. Used carelessly, it creates resistance. The difference is tone, timing, and trust.

Reaching the "why" beneath the "what"

Moving from surface concerns to deeper meaning often depends on more than a single question. It takes a thoughtful sequence that builds trust and invites reflection. Some advisors use a simple tool we call the Insight Ladder, a conversational rhythm that gently guides prospects from facts to values.

It starts with an open-ended question, something straightforward like, "What's your biggest concern about retirement?" That's the first rung, naming the worry. But the power comes in the follow-up. Asking, "Why is that important to you?" or "What makes that a top priority?" invites the prospect to connect the concern to something deeper. The follow-up question creates space for the prospect to reflect, often uncovering motivations that aren't immediately visible. Facts start to take shape as values. Worries become windows into what really matters.

Sometimes that second question opens everything. Other times, a softer approach works better: "Tell me more about what's behind that," or "What's driving that for you?" The wording can shift, but the goal is the same, creating space for reflection and revealing the motivations that guide financial choices.

"How can I help you?"

One common opening question advisors like to ask is, "How can I help you?" On the surface, it sounds warm and empathetic, even generous. But this question is more flawed than it appears.

First, it centers the advisor rather than the client. By leading with *I*, the question subtly reorients the conversation around the advisor's role, availability, and usefulness. The prospect is asked to engage with *you* before they've even clarified what *they* are thinking, wanting, or concerned about. Instead of opening space for the prospect's reality, it puts them in the position of needing to articulate how you fit into their picture, when, more often than not, they're still trying to form that picture themselves.

Second, this question assumes a level of clarity that many prospects don't yet have. It presumes they understand both the nature of their concern and the breadth of ways an experienced advisor might help. But that's rarely the case. Most prospects arrive with a mix of vague unease, partial questions, and tentative priorities. They may not yet have the language, or the confidence, to name what's most important.

So while "How can I help you?" sounds helpful, it often falls flat in practice. It invites a canned answer or forces the prospect into a premature role: that of a client who already knows what they want and how to ask for it.

A more skillful question begins where the prospect actually is. What are they noticing about their financial concerns or aspirations right now? What have they been thinking about lately? What's prompted them to have this conversation today? These types of questions locate the prospect in their own experience, and from there, the conversation can build.

Phrasing difficult questions with care

Even a powerful question can fall flat if phrased poorly. Tone matters. Timing matters. Word choice matters. Instead of "Why did you do that?" try "What led you to that decision?" Instead of "You should consider …" try "I've seen others find success with …." Reframe challenges as invitations: "Are you sure that's the right plan?" becomes "Would you be open to exploring a few other options?"

And when emotions run high, shift the timeline. "What mistakes have you made?" becomes "If you could go back 10 years, what would you do differently?" Good questions feel safe. Great ones bring agency to the prospect.

Bringing it into the room

You don't need to change your entire approach to improve discovery. Start by asking better questions. Before your next meeting, review a recorded conversation. How many of your questions invited real reflection rather than simply collecting facts? Then, prepare three open-ended questions in advance. When you ask, give the question space. Pause for a full three seconds. Let the prospect think.

It's easy to unintentionally rush this moment. Many advisors stack questions, firing off two or three in a row without waiting for a response. It might sound like, "What's most important to you about retirement? Is it freedom? Time with family?" That overloads the prospect and short-circuits real reflection. Ask one question. Then stop. Let silence carry some of the weight.

One final challenge: change one question in your next meeting. Replace a fact-finding prompt with one that invites reflection. Then watch what happens. That moment when the prospect stops reacting and starts thinking is where real discovery begins.

Thoughts to carry forward

1. Closed-ended questions trigger reflex and shut down engagement, while open-ended questions invite reflection, emotional honesty, and deeper insight.

2. When prospects pause to think, they move from rehearsed answers to personal truth, and that's where real trust and transformation begin.

3. Techniques like asking follow-up questions, careful phrasing, and reflective silence help advisors surface values and turn conversations into moments of meaningful discovery.

18

DEMONSTRATING TRUE COMPETENCE

Leading Without Dominating

Without connection, competence fades.

Warmth opens the door; competence earns the seat at the table. But here's the catch: advisors who are technically brilliant can still lose the prospect if their delivery doesn't match the prospect's emotional state. Demonstrating competence isn't about switching modes, but about deepening trust through timely, human-centered expertise.

Many advisors understand the importance of building trust before showcasing their expertise. But once that's in place, a new question arises: How do you demonstrate competence in a way that reinforces the relationship, rather than undermining it?

Sometimes, advisors hold back their expertise for too long, leaving prospects uncertain about their abilities. Or they present their knowledge too aggressively, overwhelming the prospect and weakening the relationship. The real skill lies not only in timing, but in making competence feel natural, relevant, and centered on the prospect.

What lands before logic

Before people care about what you know, they're already scanning for something else, something quieter, but more powerful: Do I feel at ease with this person? Are they genuinely here with me? We saw earlier that emotional tone comes first. That early read, how you carry yourself, how you listen, whether you rush or settle, does more to open the conversation than any credential ever will. In a high-stakes meeting, warmth is much more than a "soft skill." It's the gatekeeper.

Prospects may understand you're qualified. If they don't feel it's about them, none of it matters. Even the most technically skilled advisors will struggle to be heard if the emotional foundation isn't solid. When people don't feel safe, insight gets filtered out. Trust is the filter that allows competence to land.

Prospects won't fully engage until they feel understood. Timing and relevance matter as much as expertise. And a steady, grounded presence keeps people open. When advisors lead with technical strength before building connection, they often lose the prospect before the relationship has a chance to begin. The most effective advisors understand that trust isn't built on facts alone. It starts with emotional safety, and from there, everything else can grow.

How advisors demonstrate expertise without overwhelming

Many advisors mistakenly believe that demonstrating competence means talking more, explaining more, or proving more. In real life, the most effective advisors show their expertise through strategic communication, thoughtful framing, and well-timed insights.

Many advisors feel the urge to convince prospects of their expertise. But competence is often best communicated through a well-structured approach. When the steps are transparent and thoughtfully paced, the process itself becomes a quiet signal of confidence and care. A well-structured process speaks louder than credentials or jargon. It shows confidence, care, and experience.

It begins by clarifying the prospect's concerns with a question like, "What are your biggest financial questions right now?" From there, the advisor can explain their approach: "Here's how I typically handle situations like yours." And finally, they outline what comes next: "If we were to work together, here's what we would do first." This kind of conversation positions the advisor as a guide, not a salesperson. It reduces pressure and makes the path forward feel clear, grounded, and easy to take.

Why it matters to begin with what's already on their mind

When you start by naming what's already on their mind, you're doing more than being polite. You're being strategic. It shifts the dynamic from transactional to relational. Rather than leading with your own agenda, you're aligning with what's already alive for them. Engaging in conversations where individuals feel heard and understood can lead to neural synchrony, a phenomenon where the brain activity of the speaker and listener becomes aligned. This synchronization is associated with mutual understanding and empathy, facilitating deeper connections between individuals.

Most prospects enter a conversation carrying something: an unresolved question, a private worry, a quiet hope. If you steer too quickly toward your own content, you create friction. But when you start by getting the prospect to name what's already on their mind, whether it's the pressure of a looming decision, uncertainty about timing, or a desire for clarity, you lower resistance and raise receptivity.

This approach is empathy in motion. You're listening with the intent to meet them where they are. Not only to hear, but to understand and respond from their frame of reference. And that moment of alignment becomes the gateway to deeper trust and collaboration.

The competence-conversation sequence

Advisors who rush to demonstrate value often miss the moment to make it matter. Competence lands best when it follows the natural rhythm of trust, one that unfolds in real time. This isn't about delivering a polished script. It's about moving in sync with the client's actual experience.

It starts with their concerns and aspirations. Begin with what's already on their mind. What's keeping them up at night? What are they hoping for? These questions do more than gather information. They show that you care about where they're coming from.

Next, reflect back what you've heard. Not by repeating their words, but by paraphrasing with precision and care. When you capture their concern in your own language and they nod in recognition, that's the moment of alignment.

Only then do you affirm your ability to help. A quiet statement like, "That's something I've worked through with clients before," shows you're prepared. You're not jumping into solutions. You're showing that you've been listening and you're ready. This sequence doesn't dilute your expertise; it earns the moment to share it. When timed well, your insight won't feel like a pitch. It will feel like the natural next step.

We'll explore the psychology behind this more deeply in *The Three Silent Questions*. For now, think of it as trust's choreography: ask, align, then advise.

Providing small wins in the meeting

One of the most quietly persuasive ways to demonstrate expertise is to offer immediate value, even before a prospect officially becomes a client. A single useful insight, something they can use right away, often goes further than a detailed plan. For example, if a prospect shares concerns about taxes in retirement, the advisor might respond:

> *"I noticed something in what you shared. There may be a way to calibrate your withdrawal strategy so that you lower your tax burden. Would you like me to walk you through how that works?"*

This brief moment makes expertise tangible. The prospect doesn't simply hear about the advisor's value. They feel it in action.

Telling stories that illustrate expertise

Stories often reach people in ways statistics can't. When an advisor shares a narrative that reflects the prospect's own situation, the value becomes tangible. Listing credentials has its place, but competence often resonates more clearly when it's demonstrated through relevant, well-told stories.

Consider an advisor saying, "I recently worked with a couple in a similar situation. They were concerned about whether their savings would last, especially with market volatility. We structured a plan that reduced risk while still allowing for growth. Now, they feel much more confident about their retirement."

That kind of story does more than convey technical skill. It builds trust by showing the prospect that their concerns are understood and solvable. In this frame, expertise speaks for itself.

Letting competence land naturally

Competence and warmth are not opposites. They work in tandem. But the order matters. In the early moments of a discovery meeting, prospects are tuning into emotional cues. They're asking themselves, *Do I feel comfortable with this person?* When advisors lead with rapport, they create the emotional safety needed for expertise to be received.

Once trust starts to take root, technical skill can enter the conversation more naturally. For some, that shift happens within minutes. For others, it takes longer. And in situations where urgency drives the agenda, like a looming tax deadline or an unexpected inheritance, competence may need to step forward sooner. The key is knowing how to read the moment. Expertise involves not only knowing the answers but also recognizing when and how to introduce them into the conversation.

Demonstrating, not declaring, expertise

Advisors often make the mistake of trying to prove their value with credentials, charts, or a flood of information. Information becomes meaningful when it's relevant to the prospect's context, which is what helps build trust. When advisors frame data inside a narrative, they turn complexity into clarity. A simple statement like, "Many of my clients have found that even a small alteration, like reducing their withdrawal rate by 1–2%, can significantly extend the longevity of their retirement savings," is easier to digest, and more likely to land, than a chart on sequence-of-returns risk.

Common pitfalls include dominating the conversation, overloading the prospect with numbers, or brushing past their concerns. These habits, while often well-intentioned, can backfire. Listening more than speaking, keeping data tightly focused, and responding thoughtfully to concerns all reinforce credibility without feeling performative.

Competence speaks quietly. It becomes visible through useful insight, clear explanations, and well-timed stories that reflect the prospect's needs and concerns. When prospects feel your skill in action, they're far more likely to trust it.

Thoughts to carry forward

1. Context beats credentials. Don't lead with your designations. Lead with how your expertise applies to their concern.
2. Ask before advising. Before sharing an analysis or strategy, ask: "Would it help if I walked you through how I've helped someone in a similar situation?"
3. Let stories speak louder than stats. Let the story carry the weight. Show what it's like when the knot in someone's stomach finally loosens.

19

THE FEE CONVERSATION

When and How to Discuss Pricing
With Confidence

Why the fee conversation matters

Plenty of advisors hold back when it comes to talking about fees, afraid it might create tension. But it's usually the silence that does the damage. Openness earns confidence. When fees are unclear, prospects feel uneasy. When brought up too late, skepticism grows. But when you lead with openness and conviction, the conversation strengthens trust.

The key is timing, framing, and confidence. Too early feels transactional. Too late introduces doubt. When done right, the fee conversation makes prospects feel informed and confident, more likely to move forward.

When to discuss fees

Fee conversations can be tricky, and timing matters. Some advisors bring up fees right away, worried that delaying the topic might seem evasive. Others wait until the very end, hoping that rapport will soften the cost. But both approaches can create friction.

Introducing fees too early can make the meeting feel transactional, cutting off deeper conversation before it begins. Waiting too long can backfire too, especially if the prospect feels they have to ask. That moment can create discomfort or doubt. And vague promises about *value* without specifics often leave people more confused than confident.

The key is to be transparent without being abrupt. Introduce fees once there's enough context for the prospect to understand what they're paying for, and why it matters.

The better approach

Discuss fees after the prospect has shared what's truly on their mind, and after you've clearly stated your ability to help them. Say it plainly. This earns trust and creates a natural opening to talk about your fees.

Example:

> *"You mentioned that you're unsure if you'll have enough to retire comfortably. That's a concern I work with all the time. I want you to know that I can*

help you address this, and we'll work through it together. Let me walk you through how my fees work so you can see how this all fits."

If someone asks about fees early:

"That's a great question. I'll discuss our fees in detail, but first I want to understand what matters most to you."

How to discuss fees with confidence

When discussing fees, confidence starts with clarity. Avoid abstract claims about value and focus instead on the specific services you provide, services that directly support your prospect's financial well-being. Saying, "We provide holistic financial planning that adds long-term value," might sound polished, but it rarely makes a real impact. A more effective approach sounds like this: "Our service includes portfolio management, tax efficiency planning, retirement strategy, and risk management. These elements help grow wealth and reduce risk."

Clear language matters. Prospects value straightforward explanations, not industry jargon. It's better to say, "We charge 1.5 percent of the assets we manage for you," than "Our fee is 150 basis points." Simplicity builds trust.

If you use a tiered fee structure, present it in a way that's easy to follow. As an added touch of confidence and candor, present your fees in relation to your competitors:

For accounts around $500,000, many firms charge between 1.25 and 1.75 percent. We charge 1.50. For accounts near $1 million, the range is typically 1.00 to 1.50 percent. Our fee is 1.25. And for accounts above $2 million, where most firms fall between 0.75 and 1.25 percent, we offer 1.00.

This kind of transparency removes confusion and reinforces that your pricing is both competitive and easy to understand.

The five essentials for a strong fee discussion

A strong fee conversation rests on five essentials, each designed to build clarity and trust. It begins with leadership. Rather than waiting for the prospect to bring it up, take the initiative with a question like, "Would it be helpful to go over how our fees work?"

Next, focus on services, not vague value statements. Be specific: "We help reduce taxes, optimize retirement withdrawals, and align your investments with your long-term goals." Even better, tie your expertise to the concern they've already voiced. If they're worried about running out of money, you might say, "We create a withdrawal strategy designed to prevent that exact problem that you're concerned about." This helps the prospect link your fee directly to the relief of their most pressing worry, whether they realize it consciously or not.

And when it comes to the numbers, keep it clear and simple. For example, "Our fees range from 1.25 to 1.5 percent, depending on the size of your portfolio." Context matters too. Help the prospect understand how your pricing compares by saying something like, "Most firms charge between 1.25 and 1.75 percent. Our fee includes both planning and full portfolio management." Finally, put everything in writing. A concise, one-page summary reinforces transparency and helps prevent future misunderstandings.

Handling common fee objections

Even with the right timing and tone, some prospects will hesitate when it comes to fees. The key is to respond with composed assurance, not defensiveness. Below are three common objections, along with effective ways to respond.

Objection: "I can get this cheaper somewhere else."

Response: That's possible. But lower fees often come with fewer services, less expertise, and more time spent figuring things out on your own. Our fee includes comprehensive planning, tax strategy, and ongoing support. It's meant to support the life you're building, not only the assets you're managing.

Objection: "What exactly do I get for this fee?"

Response: You get more than a financial plan. You get a partner. We manage your portfolio, optimize your taxes, plan for retirement, and assess risk. And we stay in touch with regular check-ins and updates that adjust with your life. This is a full-service relationship, not a one-time transaction.

Objection: "Why should I pay when I can use an online service?"

Response: Algorithms invest. We advise. From taxes to retirement, your full financial picture gets human attention.

Or:

Platforms invest your money. We help you plan your life: taxes, estate, retirement, and everything in between.

Making it natural

The best advisors don't stop at clarifying fees. They show what those fees make possible. They make the conversation feel natural and grounded. They show why the investment is worth it by connecting it directly to the services provided and the prospect's specific concerns. That means being proactive. Rather than waiting for the question, they introduce the topic with calm confidence. They anchor their fees not only to portfolio management or planning, but to the outcomes that matter most to the client, such as reducing taxes, easing decision fatigue, or increasing long-term security.

Language matters here. Speak plainly and avoid jargon. A straightforward explanation goes further than polished phrasing. Reinforce your transparency by putting it in writing, ideally a one-page summary that's easy to review and refer back to. And above all, hold the conversation with steady confidence. When you approach fees as a normal part of a clear, respectful process, your client will too.

Thoughts to carry forward

1. Discussing fees clearly and confidently, after outlining your services but before the meeting ends, builds trust and increases the likelihood of client conversion.
2. Avoid jargon and vague value statements; instead, use plain language and specific examples to explain what the fee covers, ideally supported by a simple visual breakdown.
3. Reinforce that the fee isn't tied to transactions. It's tied to long-term partnership and ongoing guidance.

20
TECH WITHOUT THE TALK

Using Tools Without Losing Touch

The risk of opening with software

Andrés, a seasoned advisor, liked being prepared. In his discovery meetings, he opened with confidence: a polished agenda, a complex tax report, a perfectly tuned software walkthrough. Fifteen minutes into this one, the prospect had barely spoken. They smiled politely, nodded occasionally, but their body language said something else, hands still, gaze flicking between screen and advisor, a hesitation in every response.

Andrés realized they hadn't asked a single question. They weren't lost. They were disconnected. He'd led with tools instead of trust.

In discovery meetings, software is part of the landscape. But when it dominates the room, it can flatten the conversation. Tools should support insight, not replace human connection. Andrés knew the math. But in that moment, what he needed was curiosity. The key? Talk first. Tech second.

When to let the numbers speak

Many advisors start discovery with a screen share, assuming that competence means leading with data. But in reality, it is warmth, not numbers, that earns the right to advise. Leading with curiosity creates a very different kind of opening. Instead of saying, "Let me show you a tax projection for different withdrawal strategies," consider asking, "When you think about taxes in retirement, what's your biggest concern?" This small shift moves the conversation from presentation to dialogue. Prospects engage emotionally first and logically second. The numbers should support the conversation, not control it.

Once the relationship is grounded, visuals can help make the future feel more concrete. Simple, focused tech use adds clarity, especially when adjusted in real time. For example: "Let's see what happens if you claim Social Security at 62 versus 67. Which scenario feels more aligned with your goals?" A visual placed with intent turns raw data into something the client can envision and act on.

From there, the advisor's role is to translate numbers into meaning. Most prospects aren't concerned with how the software works. They care what it means for their lives. A simple framework helps. Show the numbers, explain them in plain language, then connect the insight to a real decision.

For instance: "This shows that if you withdraw from your taxable account first, you may reduce your overall lifetime tax burden by $80,000. Would you like to explore this further?"

Timing is essential. The most effective use of technology comes *after* the prospect has shared their concerns. Leading with software too early can short-circuit connection. A better flow starts with a question, "What's your biggest worry about retirement income?" then introduces the tool as a way to explore together: "Let's take a quick look at that." Keep it collaborative: "What if we adjusted this? How does that feel?" When advisors jump into tech too quickly, as Andrés did, the problem isn't the software, it's the timing. Used at the right moment, technology doesn't replace the conversation. It deepens it.

Common tech missteps, and how to fix them

Technology can strengthen a discovery conversation. Or it can quietly disrupt it. One common misstep is offering too much data too quickly. Handing over a twelve-page tax report early in the meeting can overwhelm rather than support understanding. A better approach might be, "Let's compare two strategies visually so you can see the impact." A focused visual keeps the discussion grounded and digestible.

Another challenge is letting the software do the talking. When an advisor clicks through screens while the prospect watches in silence, the meeting shifts from dialogue to demonstration. Instead, pause and ask, "What are you thinking when you see this?" That question re-engages the prospect and turns the moment into a conversation.

Tool overload is another easy trap. Switching between multiple programs in a single meeting can leave people confused and disconnected. A more effective approach is to focus on the one tool that directly addresses their top concern. That clarity keeps the meeting productive and reinforces trust.

Keep software in service to the story

Technology can elevate your discovery meetings, but only when it follows your curiosity, not your agenda. Advisors who lead with empathy and ask better questions find that software becomes a bridge, not a barrier.

Use tech to highlight, not hijack. Keep the screen behind the scenes until the prospect feels heard. Then, and only then, bring it forward to help them visualize options and explore decisions in real time. Used this way, software clarifies rather than overwhelms. And the result? Conversations that build rapport, invite honesty, and earn the right to advise.

Thoughts to carry forward

1. Leading with software can alienate prospects. Start with human connection, not data.
2. Use technology sparingly and interactively to clarify, not dominate, the conversation.
3. When software serves the story, it strengthens rapport and reveals deeper priorities.

21
LEADING DISCOVERY IN A DIGITAL WORLD

Staying Human Across Any Format

Redesigning rapport for a virtual world

In the past, financial advisors leaned on the rhythms of in-person meetings to build trust, firm handshakes, shared space, subtle cues. But the landscape has shifted. Virtual and hybrid meetings are now part of the norm, and many advisors are left asking: Can connection still come through a screen?

It can. But it doesn't happen by accident. Building rapport in a virtual setting depends less on adopting new tools and more on using familiar ones with greater intention. Eye contact, vocal tone, posture, presence, these signals still matter, but they need to be amplified to register. Prospects notice everything, from your lighting and background to the way your energy carries through the screen. A cluttered visual or a flat tone can undermine your message. Handled thoughtfully, virtual meetings can match the connection of face-to-face and occasionally uncover even more. The relationship isn't built in the room anymore. It's built in the frame.

Creating impact on the screen

Making an impression on screen starts with how you show up, not simply that you do. Presence isn't about being visible. It's about being fully engaged, even through a lens. Look into the camera instead of at your screen to simulate eye contact. Modulate your voice with warmth and clarity, allowing your tone and pacing to bring energy into the conversation. Even subtle body language, like a nod, a soft smile, or a slight lean forward, can help communicate attentiveness and connection. These small cues matter, especially in a medium where so much is filtered.

Your setup also carries weight. A clean, uncluttered background conveys professionalism. A quality microphone brings richness to your voice, making you sound more engaged and trustworthy. These aren't purely aesthetic choices. In a virtual setting, they shape how you're perceived.

One of the simplest but most powerful habits in virtual meetings is the three-second pause. Without the natural cues of in-person interaction, silence tends to feel longer on screen. Many advisors rush to fill that space. But by pausing for three full seconds after a prospect finishes speaking, you create room for something deeper. It may feel awkward at first, but that space often prompts people to say more, sometimes revealing what they didn't plan to share. In that pause, new insight often emerges.

Finally, language matters more than ever in a virtual setting, where tone can carry more weight than body language. A question that feels neutral in person can come across as pointed on screen. Consider softening your phrasing. Instead of asking, "Why did you decide to work with your current advisor?" try "Can you walk me through how you chose your advisor and what mattered most to you?" Or, rather than asking, "What are your financial concerns?" ask, "What would peace of mind look like for you?"

These subtle shifts create a sense of safety, and safety opens the door to honesty. On screen, every word and pause carries a little more weight. The more intentionally you use them, the more trust you earn.

From adjustment to advantage

Virtual meetings have changed the landscape of discovery conversations, offering new ways for advisors to lead with greater precision and presence. Those who master digital body language, ask with empathy, and let silence do some of the work are the ones who stand out. They're not filling a square, they're shaping the experience. They use the medium intentionally, creating real rapport no matter where the conversation takes place.

Start small. Record your next virtual discovery meeting and watch it from the prospect's perspective. Practice the three-second pause. Wait long enough for something real to surface. Change one thing, your camera angle, your tone, or the way you phrase a question, and see what shifts in response.

Connection hasn't disappeared. It's moved to a new home. Advisors who adapt to that reality position themselves to connect more effectively in a changing landscape.

Thoughts to carry forward

1. In virtual or hybrid meetings, meaningful connection requires conscious choices, not default behavior.
2. Advisors must adapt their cues: eye contact, voice tone, pauses, and question phrasing, to recreate warmth and credibility through the screen.
3. Success in discovery now depends on fluency across formats, with flexibility and reflection becoming strategic advantages.

PART FOUR

Adapting to the Person in Front of You

No two prospects are alike. What builds trust with one might create friction with another. Discovery mastery isn't defined by the right questions alone. It's about reading the room, adjusting your presence, and staying grounded in who you are while flexing to meet the person in front of you. This section helps you shift from a fixed approach to a responsive one. Because when prospects feel truly seen, they open up. And that changes everything.

Chapters in this section

22

- **Adapting Discovery for Different Prospect Types:** Meeting People Where They Are
- **The Three Silent Questions:** What Every Prospect Is Really Assessing
- **The Sales Call You Didn't Know You Were Making:** How Discovery Shapes the Decision

ADAPTING DISCOVERY FOR DIFFERENT PROSPECT TYPES

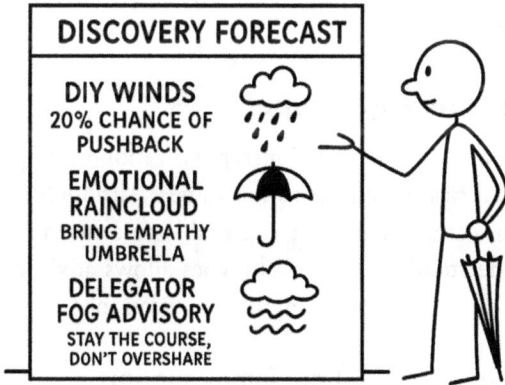

Meeting People Where They Are

Personalizing discovery to meet the moment

No two prospects arrive the same way. Some want numbers, charts, and efficiency. Others are searching for reassurance or clarity. One might be ready to dive into every financial detail, while another is hoping to delegate most of the work. Some arrive with spreadsheets. Others feel overwhelmed and unsure where to begin.

Advisors rely on familiar questions and conversational cues, but they adapt in the moment. That's why rigid, one-size-fits-all discovery processes often fall short. They can crowd out the flexibility needed to follow what truly matters. Some prospects will disengage if the conversation gets too technical. Others may feel frustrated if it lingers too long on emotion. Preferences around pace, depth, and decision-making vary, and those differences shape how trust is built.

What you ask, and how you ask, matters. The more attuned you are to the person in front of you, their mindset, comfort level, and communication style, the more useful, engaging, and effective discovery becomes. Personalization isn't extra. It's the work.

Nine key discovery archetypes

Every prospect has a unique relationship with money, shaped by life experiences, financial history, and personal values. Although every prospect is unique, advisors often encounter recognizable patterns in how people relate to money. Understanding these archetypes allows advisors to tailor their approach for deeper, more meaningful conversations.

1. The solo ager: aging without family support

Solo agers do not have immediate family to assist them as they grow older. Their financial concerns often center on long-term care, financial security, and who will advocate for them if they experience cognitive decline. Unlike prospects with strong family ties, they lack built-in support systems, making them more vulnerable to financial mismanagement and isolation.

Discovery should ensure these prospects have a decision-making plan for later years. This includes discussing estate planning, power of attorney, and long-term care options. Many solo agers also need guidance on fraud prevention, as they are often targets for financial scams.

A simple but powerful question:

"Who will you rely on most as you age?"

2. The high-income analytical prospect: data-driven and results-oriented

This prospect views financial planning through a logical, numbers-driven lens. Often professionals or executives, they prioritize efficiency and measurable results. Emotional storytelling is unlikely to resonate. They want data, models, and clear explanations of risk and reward.

These clients respond well to clear visuals, scenario analysis, and performance metrics. Keep conversations structured and concise. Emphasize the tangible value of financial planning.

A key question:

"What data or insights would help you feel confident about our process?"

3. The emotionally driven prospect: seeking trust and reassurance

Some clients make financial decisions based more on emotion than logic. Advisors must establish trust before diving into numbers. Rushing into strategies or technical detail can backfire if fears are unresolved. Discovery should focus on emotional triggers, past experiences, and what financial security means to them.

A thoughtful question:

"What worries you most about your financial future?"

4. The delegator: prefers a hands-off approach

Some prospects want an advisor to handle their finances end-to-end. They value financial planning but aren't interested in managing the details. With this group, focus on demonstrating competence and reliability. They want confidence their finances are handled, without being involved in every decision.

A clarifying question:

"What level of involvement do you prefer in managing your finances?"

5. The DIY investor: skeptical but curious

These prospects have managed their own investments and may question the value of an advisor. They often see advisors as an expense rather than an asset. Take a collaborative approach. Instead of taking control, highlight areas they might not have considered, like tax efficiency, risk management, or behavioral coaching.

A useful question:

"What would have to happen for you to see value in working with an advisor?"

6. The sudden wealth recipient: overwhelmed by new responsibilities

Clients who have recently come into wealth often feel anxious, unprepared, or even guilty. Here, the advisor's role is to bring structure and reassurance. Keep the conversation step-by-step to avoid overwhelm while helping them build a foundation.

A grounding question:

"What's your biggest concern about managing this new wealth?"

7. The overwhelmed caregiver: balancing family and finances

Some prospects are caring for aging parents while raising children. Financially stretched and emotionally drained, they often struggle to prioritize their own goals. Advisors can help by guiding them to set financial boundaries and make guilt-free decisions. Topics should include long-term care, college funding, and retirement planning.

A supportive question:

"How do you see your financial role within your family, and what worries you most about it?"

8. The crisis-driven prospect: reacting, not planning

These clients come to the table during a crisis: job loss, divorce, illness, or business failure. Their thinking is short-term and emotionally charged. The advisor's job is to help them regain control and shift from reactive to proactive. First, stabilize their current financial situation. Then, introduce long-term planning.

A grounding question:

> *"What financial decisions feel most urgent to you right now, and what has led to this point?"*

9. The values-based investor: prioritizing purpose over profits

Some prospects see money as a means to create change. They care about philanthropy, sustainability, or faith-driven investing. Discovery should uncover their deeper motivations. Be ready to explore socially responsible investing, charitable strategies, and estate planning aligned with their values.

A meaningful question:

> *"What impact do you want your wealth to have, both for your family and the world?"*

Adapting in real time

Even the best-planned discovery meeting won't always go as expected. Prospects may shift in and out of different archetypes, depending on their emotions or circumstances. Advisors should stay alert for non-verbal cues, hesitation, or disengagement, and be ready to modify their approach on the fly.

Discovery reveals how a person thinks about their finances, and what truly matters to them. It's a way of seeing how a person thinks, what they value, and what drives their decisions. Great advisors don't lead the conversation. They move with it. They listen for what's said, and what's not, then adapt in real time. Advisors who meet prospects in both their situation and their state of mind turn routine moments into real relationships.

Thoughts to carry forward

1. Discovery thrives on adaptability. One-size-fits-all approaches fall short because every prospect brings a different mindset, emotion, and level of engagement.

2. Knowing prospect archetypes helps advisors tailor conversations that build trust, reduce overwhelm, and meet each person where they are.

3. Great advisors adjust in real time, recognizing emotional cues and shifting their approach to deepen connection and clarity.

23

THE THREE
SILENT QUESTIONS

What Every Prospect Is Really Asking

What your prospects are thinking but won't tell you

Years of training go into mastering the financial advisory craft. But most prospects don't respond to mastery, they respond to moments that feel personal, relevant, and real. First, advisors must establish a genuine connection. Then, they must demonstrate their expertise in a way that reinforces confidence rather than undermining it.

Let's look at the silent process prospects follow before saying yes to working with an advisor. While they may not verbalize it, every prospect is subconsciously evaluating three fundamental questions:

- Do I like you?
- Do I trust you?
- Do I believe you have the competence to help me solve my issue?

These questions form a kind of decision pyramid. Likeability forms the base, trust builds the middle, and perceived competence completes the top. Skip a layer, and the whole structure wobbles. This *three questions* framework is grounded in decades of research showing that we evaluate warmth before expertise. In other words, people decide how they feel about you before they care how much you know. For financial advisors, that means you must first be perceived as likeable and trustworthy before your expertise will truly resonate.

1. Do I like this advisor? (The warmth factor)

Likeability has less to do with being impressive and more to do with being easy to be around. Many advisors lead with their credentials, assuming expertise will carry the room. But prospects aren't asking, "Are you smart?" They're asking, "Do I feel comfortable with you?"

First impressions form quickly and are difficult to reverse. To be perceived as likeable, an advisor should:

- Open with curiosity, not credentials. Ask about the prospect's situation before jumping into your process.
- Listen more than you speak. Use follow-ups like, "Can you tell me more about that?" or "How has that impacted you?"

- Match their tone and energy. A nervous prospect may need reassurance, while a confident one may appreciate efficiency.

A strong opening (after a few minutes of small talk) might sound like this:

> *"Before we get going, I'd love to hear what's been weighing on you financially. What made you reach out?"*

This immediately shifts the focus to the prospect, not the advisor.

Important note: *When asking this question to a couple, make sure you hear from both partners. If one person takes the lead, listen fully. Then turn to the quieter partner and ask the same question directly. (Avoid asking, "Do you agree?")*

2. Do I trust this advisor? (The connection factor)

Trust isn't something prospects evaluate explicitly. It builds gradually, through listening, presence, and the feeling that their concerns are understood. Many advisors assume that technical expertise is the foundation for trust. But in practice, what often matters more is how well the advisor listens, responds, and makes space for what the client is actually carrying.

You've probably heard the quote often linked to Theodore Roosevelt: "People don't care how much you know until they know how much you care." It remains relevant because it points to something enduring. Information alone doesn't move people. What does is the experience of being cared for and taken seriously. Trust begins when the prospect senses both.

So how do you build that trust? Start by uncovering the concern that brought them in. Ask directly, "What's the financial issue that led you to reach out?" Then reflect back what you've heard to confirm that you're on the same page: "So if I'm hearing you right, your biggest concern is ensuring your retirement income will last. Is that right?"

The next step is to resist the impulse to jump into solutions. Slow down. Invite them to share more: "You mentioned you're feeling uncertain about your income lasting through retirement. Can you say more about what specifically feels unclear or unsettling?" These questions don't stop at listening. They lay the groundwork for trust, where real advice can land and stick.

3. Do I believe this advisor has the competence to help me solve my issue? (The competence factor)

Competence matters, but it rarely lands without trust. Many advisors try to prove their expertise too early, hoping credentials or insights will win confidence. But prospects aren't evaluating facts in isolation, they're responding to how well they feel understood.

The turning point often comes when they hear their own concerns reflected back with accuracy and care. At that moment, the question shifts from "Can you help me?" to something more settled, "You already are."

Competence shows up most clearly when the advisor can summarize the problem in the client's language, share how similar situations have been handled, and describe a process that feels tailored to what the client actually needs, not a generic template.

For example: "It sounds like you're wondering whether you've saved enough to retire comfortably, and you're uncertain whether your current plan offers the security you want. That's exactly what we help clients with. Based on what you've shared, we'd take a three-part approach. First, we look closely at your income needs and spending expectations. Second, we stress-test your portfolio across a range of retirement scenarios. And third, we build a strategy to help ensure your income stays reliable over time. Does that sound like what you're looking for?"

When framed this way, competence doesn't need to be declared, it's demonstrated through clarity, relevance, and a calm sense of direction.

Applying the three questions in a meeting: role-play scenario

Scenario: A couple seeking retirement clarity

Background: Warren and Michael have scheduled a discovery meeting. They've worked hard to save for retirement but feel uncertain about their readiness. Conflicting advice online has left them overwhelmed and looking for clarity.

Step 1: Opening—building likeability and trust

Advisor: "It's great to meet you both. Before we dive into the details, I'd love to hear what led you to reach out. What's been on your mind when it comes to your finances?"

Warren: "We're both planning to retire in the next few years, but we don't know if we have enough saved."

Michael: "We keep seeing different advice online. Some say you need a million, others say it varies. We're trying to understand what's true for us."

Step 2: Listening and deepening trust

Advisor: "I hear you. Retirement planning advice can feel all over the place, and it's frustrating when you're trying to make big decisions. If I understand correctly, your biggest concern is knowing whether your savings will last. Does that sound right?"

Warren and Michael: "Yes! You've hit the nail on the head."

Step 3: Demonstrating competence without overwhelming

Advisor: "That makes perfect sense, and you're not alone in feeling this way. Here's how we typically approach this:

1. We start by reviewing your current assets, spending needs, and retirement goals.
2. Next, we run projections to see how different scenarios could affect your income over time.
3. Finally, we look at any calibrations that might strengthen your plan. Would that kind of analysis be helpful for you?"

Warren: "Yep. That's exactly what we've been wanting to hear."

Thoughts to carry forward

1. Before deciding to move forward, prospects subconsciously evaluate advisors by asking three core questions: Do I like you? Do I trust you? Do I believe you can help me?
2. Advisors don't earn trust with credentials. They earn it by listening, showing empathy, and matching the prospect's tone.
3. Competence should be demonstrated last and shown through personalized insight, clear process, and relevance to the prospect's situation, not through technical explanations alone.

24

THE SALES CALL YOU DIDN'T KNOW YOU WERE MAKING

How Discovery Shapes the Decision

When discovery becomes a decision moment

Most advisors don't see themselves as salespeople, and for good reason. Their role is rooted in guidance, problem-solving, and professional expertise. They're not in the business of pushing products or closing quick deals. The old-school pitch doesn't fit, and most know it.

Still, there's a tension. Even if you don't call it a sales call, a discovery meeting often follows the same rhythm. The advisor leads the structure. The conversation gradually moves toward a decision. And much of the airtime is spent explaining, educating, and reinforcing value. It may sound more polished than a hard pitch. It may feel more collaborative. But in practice, it still functions like a sales conversation. The difference is in tone, not intention.

The real obstacle: inertia, not other firms

Advisors often assume their biggest competitor is another firm. Maybe the one down the street, an online platform, or the prospect's current provider. But in reality, the greatest obstacle is usually something quieter and harder to spot: inertia.

Most prospects aren't resisting because they doubt your value. They're hesitating because the path forward feels uncertain. The options can seem unclear. The complexity feels overwhelming. And even when they recognize the limitations of their current setup, emotional attachment can make it hard to let go.

It's not that change doesn't make sense. It's that change doesn't feel comfortable. That hesitation has less to do with logic and more to do with what it takes to step into something unfamiliar.

The psychology of decision-making: why prospects freeze

Understanding the psychology behind inaction helps advisors lead discovery conversations that move prospects forward without pressure. Several patterns tend to show up in financial decision-making, and each plays a role in why people hesitate to make changes.

One common force is **status quo bias**. People tend to prefer what feels familiar, even when better options are available. This is less about logic and more about emotional comfort. A gentle way to explore this is to ask, "If nothing changed for the next five years, how would you feel about that?"

Loss aversion is another factor. People feel the pain of loss more intensely than the satisfaction of gain. In fact, research suggests losses are felt almost twice as strongly. Instead of saying, "You could improve your portfolio," consider asking, "What might it cost you to keep it the way it is?" This shifts the focus from abstract improvement to tangible risk.

The **endowment effect** also plays a role. People often overvalue what they already have, even if it's no longer serving them. Rather than offering direct critique, it's often more effective to say, "It looks like your current approach has served you well. What do you think could be improved?" This affirms the past while opening space for change.

Finally, **cognitive dissonance** arises when two beliefs are in conflict. For example, "I'm responsible with money" and "I haven't updated my plan in years." Rather than confronting the inconsistency, ask a question that lets it surface on its own: "How confident are you that your current strategy protects what matters most over the next 10 years?" When discovery meetings account for these internal dynamics, they become more than fact-finding sessions. They become spaces where prospects can shift from hesitation to clarity, on their own terms.

Designing discovery that leads to action, not pressure

Discovery is not about selling change. It's about helping people uncover why they might want it for themselves. That shift begins when you move from persuasion to clarity. Rather than trying to convince, ask thoughtful, open questions that give the prospect room to reflect. Questions like, "What's working well in your plan?" or "What concerns, if any, keep you up at night?" can lead to meaningful insights. Even asking, "If nothing changed, would that be okay with you?" invites quiet evaluation without pressure.

Let the prospect verbalize the problem before you suggest a solution. Instead of saying, "You need to update your strategy," try asking, "Have you thought about how taxes could impact your income?" When they name the issue, they begin to take ownership of it. That moment of recognition is often more powerful than anything you could explain.

It also helps to reframe the cost of doing nothing. Rather than promising improvement, ask, "What's at stake if you don't make a change?" This shifts the conversation from abstract upside to personal relevance.

Finally, leave the decision in their hands. Close the conversation with language that invites, rather than directs. You might ask, "What do you feel would be a good next step?" or "Would it be helpful to explore how we might work together?" Even a simple, "What timeline makes sense for you?" signals respect and collaboration.

When discovery is designed this way, it guides without pushing. And it gives the prospect something rare. Space to decide for themselves.

Advisor check-in: your process has inertia, too

It's easy to focus on a prospect's hesitation and overlook your own. But discovery isn't shaped by their mindset alone. It's shaped by yours. If your process hasn't evolved in years, that inertia may be affecting more than you realize. Ask yourself: "Are your meetings energizing or merely efficient? Are you attracting the clients you truly want, or settling for the ones who say yes? If nothing about your approach changed, where would you be five years from now? Is your process helping you shape the future, or simply react to it?"

These questions aren't meant as warnings. They're invitations. Because *good enough* is often the most comfortable place to stall. Like the clients you serve, the cost of staying the same is easy to miss, until it becomes too visible to ignore.

That's why the most effective advisors don't push. They clear the path. When a prospect begins to see, on their own, that staying the same carries more risk than moving forward, the decision no longer feels forced. It feels necessary. Pressure gives way to clarity. And the next step becomes theirs to take.

Thoughts to carry forward

1. Many advisors unknowingly structure their discovery meetings like sales calls, which can subtly trigger resistance rather than trust.
2. The real barrier to client engagement isn't competition. It's inertia, fueled by psychological forces like loss aversion and the status quo bias.
3. Advisors can overcome resistance not by persuading, but by guiding prospects to articulate their own reasons for change through clarity, reflection, and choice.

PART FIVE

After the Meeting and Beyond

Discovery doesn't end when the meeting does. In fact, what happens after can matter even more. How you follow up, how you hold the emotional arc, how you help a prospect move from clarity to commitment. All of it shapes what comes next. This section shows you how to carry the trust you've built forward. Because connection is only one part of great discovery. It's about momentum, follow-through, and creating the kind of experience that prospects want to share.

Chapters in this section

- **Redefining Success in Discovery:** Why Conversion Isn't the Only Win
- **Stay Steady:** Managing Emotional Whiplash After the First Meeting
- **The Post-Discovery Process:** Moving from Insight to Action
- **Moving from Clarity to Commitment:** Helping Prospects Say Yes to Themselves
- **How Discovery Drives Referrals and Retention:** Trust That Multiplies
- **The Tipping Point of Discovery:** Change Is Calling

25
REDEFINING SUCCESS IN DISCOVERY

Why Conversion Isn't the Only Win

Measuring what really matters in discovery

For decades, success in discovery meant two things: collect the data and close the deal. Traditionally, discovery has been treated as a step toward a sale: a structured process of gathering financial details, demonstrating expertise, and persuading prospects to move forward. But what if success is no longer defined by closing or data collection?

A more meaningful standard focuses on three elements: prospect engagement, emotional openness, and the overall quality of the conversation. These human-centered outcomes better reflect what today's clients actually want from their advisory relationships. They're more informed, more skeptical, and less willing to be "sold." What they want is to be understood.

Where the traditional model misses the mark

Many advisors still approach discovery with a transactional mindset. Focused on gathering financial data, showcasing expertise, and steering prospects toward the next step. But these well-meaning intentions often backfire.

When a meeting is structured around fact-finding, it can feel more like a checklist than a conversation. Leading with a sales pitch may cause prospects to disengage. And when advisors dominate the airtime, often speaking up to 70 percent of the time, it becomes harder for prospects to open up or feel heard. The result is a meeting that feels impersonal, rushed, and out of sync with what the prospect needs most: a chance to feel understood.

New metrics for success

A successful discovery meeting isn't measured by polish or how much data is covered. It's measured by depth, by the quality of the conversation and how it makes the prospect feel. One key signal is engagement. When a meeting is working, the prospect does most of the talking. They ask thoughtful questions, reflect aloud, and show curiosity in their tone and posture. The advisor's role is to create that space. Speak less than half the time. Frame your questions to spark stories, not simple replies.

Emotional openness is another marker. Trust deepens when a prospect feels safe enough to share more than numbers and goals. The real shift happens when they talk about their fears, their hopes, and what they believe about money and life. Ask yourself: Did the conversation go beyond logistics? Did they share something personal or unexpected? That kind of openness comes when you lead with warmth, slow the pace, and give your full attention without distraction.

Finally, the quality of the conversation matters. A high-quality meeting doesn't feel rehearsed or overly scripted. It helps the prospect clarify what actually matters to them. It opens space for bigger questions like "What would financial peace of mind look like for you?" or "What concerns keep you up at night?" When a meeting like this resonates, it informs while also opening new perspectives and bringing clarity to what matters most.

Shifting the advisor's mindset

To create discovery meetings that truly connect, advisors need to release the instinct to lead with answers. The goal isn't to convince someone to say yes. It's to understand who they are, what they care about, and what might be getting in their way.

This kind of connection requires a shift in posture. It begins with creating space, moments of pause that invite deeper reflection. It deepens when you ask follow-up questions that explore the story behind the initial response. And it holds when you resist the urge to fix or impress before you fully understand.

Leadership in discovery doesn't come from taking control. It comes from being invited in. When that happens, the conversation stops being transactional and starts becoming transformational.

Putting the new metrics into practice

Putting these new metrics into practice starts with seeing yourself clearly. Review a few of your discovery meetings (Are you recording them and/or can you get a transcript?). Notice your talk-time. Pay attention to which questions sparked deeper dialogue, and which ones seemed to stall the conversation. These small observations often reveal patterns that are easy to miss in the moment.

After each meeting, take time for honest self-assessment. Did you listen more than you spoke? Did you learn something meaningful about the prospect's values, not only their goals? Did the conversation feel human, or merely efficient?

Redefining success means shifting your focus. It's not about performance metrics. It's about relational ones. A successful meeting doesn't hinge on a flawless presentation or polished pitch. It sounds different. The prospect talks. You listen. And somewhere in that exchange, connection begins to form. Not because you sold something, but because you cared enough to understand. Advisors who adopt this mindset don't need to push to stand out. In a profession still shaped by transactional habits, presence, curiosity, and care will set them apart.

Where discovery leads

If you've made it this far in this book, you're most likely already thinking differently about discovery. This is more than data. It's the groundwork for trust and growth. The best advisors don't chase the perfect. The very best advisors rely on familiar questions and conversational cues, but they also adapt in the moment. That's why rigid, one-size-fits-all discovery processes often fall short. They can crowd out the flexibility needed to follow what truly matters. They don't chase imperfect prospects either. They focus on showing up with clarity, curiosity, and care. Keep refining. Keep listening. Keep putting the prospect first. That's where trust begins, and where success follows.

Thoughts to carry forward

1. Traditional discovery meetings prioritize closing and data collection, but these transactional goals often lead to impersonal conversations that miss what prospects value most, which is being truly understood.

2. Modern success metrics shift the focus to engagement, emotional openness, and conversational depth, allowing prospects to share more meaningfully and build genuine trust.

3. Advisors can improve by listening more than they speak, using open-ended questions, and creating reflective space, transforming discovery from a sales step into the start of a relationship.

26

STAY STEADY

Managing Emotional Whiplash
After the First Meeting

How to stay grounded when discovery gets bumpy

Financial advisors are trained to manage their clients' emotions but often overlook their own. Discovery meetings can be emotionally demanding, especially when prospects seem skeptical or disengaged. In those moments, it's easy to feel frustrated, discouraged, or even personally rejected.

Technical skill is essential, but emotional resilience is equally critical. Advisors who stay focused under pressure and adapt in the moment build stronger relationships, foster deeper engagement, and avoid burnout. Emotional steadiness reflects a practiced discipline, one that helps keep the conversation grounded, especially when stakes feel high.

Why emotional steadiness matters in discovery

The discovery meeting is a pivotal moment. It sets the tone for a potential relationship and often determines whether a prospect decides to move forward. Because the stakes feel high, these meetings can stir strong reactions. When things don't go as planned, advisors may feel self-doubt, frustration, or even defensiveness, emotions that rarely stay contained.

Neuroscience tells us that emotions are contagious. We naturally mirror the tone in the room, often without realizing it. A calm, grounded advisor helps settle a nervous client. But when tension enters the space, even subtly, it can quietly shift the energy and derail the conversation. First impressions are processed emotionally before they're evaluated logically. People notice how you speak, how you move, and how you carry yourself long before they absorb what you know. That's why emotional steadiness matters so deeply. It gives the client something to anchor to, something trustworthy.

Certain moments are more likely to trigger emotional reactions. An advisor might feel reactive when a client withholds information or hesitates to open up. Or when a prospect pushes back on a recommendation. Sometimes it's a flash of indifference from across the table, or the sting of rejection after a meeting that felt promising. These reactions are human. But left unchecked, they can steer the meeting off course.

In our research studies from the Horsesmouth Discovery Lab, advisors spoke for about 70 percent of the meeting time. In follow-up interviews, many admitted they weren't talking to add value. They were talking to fill the silence and manage their own discomfort. Recognizing these patterns is the beginning of change. Awareness opens the door to composure, and composure is what earns trust in the moments that matter most.

Composure is the real edge

High-pressure conversations often activate the brain's stress response. When that happens, it's common for advisors to react in patterned ways. Some start pushing harder to prove their value. Others rush through the agenda or skip important steps. And some simply shut down, trying to sidestep discomfort. These reactions don't appear out of nowhere. They're shaped by past experiences. An advisor who's been challenged often might become defensive. Another, eager to avoid conflict, may over-explain or shift into presentation mode.

A useful way to break these patterns is through self-audit. Ask yourself: What emotions come up when a client questions my recommendations? Do I notice myself talking more when someone seems uninterested? How do I typically respond to emotional distance? These reflections can help you recognize your default responses before they hijack the meeting.

From there, emotional reframing becomes a powerful tool. Instead of internalizing resistance or disengagement, reframing invites you to meet those moments with curiosity and steadiness. A frustrating thought like, "Why won't they engage?" becomes "What concern might be holding them back?" Instead of, "They don't trust me," try thinking, "They may need more time and clarity to feel safe." Even something as discouraging as, "This meeting is going nowhere," can shift to, "What pivot might re-engage them?"

Reframing is not about ignoring challenges. It's about interpreting them in a way that keeps you present and grounded. Over time, this mindset helps turn emotional friction into productive turning points, for both you and the prospect.

Techniques for managing reactions in real time

Once you're aware of your emotional tendencies in discovery meetings, you can start to shift them. The key is not to suppress emotion, but to manage it with presence and intention. A simple pause and a deep breath before responding can make the difference between reacting and replying with clarity. That moment of space allows you to gather your thoughts, rather than letting the heat of the moment take over.

When faced with resistance, try reframing it. Instead of interpreting skepticism as rejection, see it as a sign of curiosity, or a signal that the prospect simply needs more clarity before they can move forward. This shift in perspective can help you respond with openness rather than defensiveness.

Many advisors find the Three-Second Rule to be helpful. When asked a difficult question, take a full three seconds before answering. Let the question land. Think. Then respond. This short pause not only gives you time to collect your thoughts, it also shows the prospect that you're listening deeply and taking their concern seriously.

Another underrated but powerful practice is intentional silence. Resist the urge to fill every pause. Sometimes the most important insights surface after a moment of quiet. When you leave space, you invite reflection, and that's often when prospects reveal what's really on their minds. Staying steady in a meeting doesn't mean being unshakable. It means staying grounded and flexible, able to meet pressure with calm and clarity. That presence is what shifts you from being capable to being someone they trust.

Long-term strategies for emotional resilience

Emotional steadiness isn't built overnight. It takes time, intention, and repeated practice. One of the most effective ways to grow in this area is through regular self-debriefs. After a meeting, pause and ask yourself how you felt during key moments. What triggered those reactions? What did you handle well? What might you approach differently next time?

Setting clear emotional boundaries also matters. Letting tension carry over doesn't simply exhaust you. It limits how fully you can be there for others. That's how burnout begins.

To strengthen your composure, it helps to rehearse difficult conversations in low-stakes settings. Role-playing or simulated discussions give you the chance to build emotional endurance. With each run-through, you train yourself to stay present and grounded, even when things get uncomfortable.

And above all, adopt a mindset that sees difficult meetings not as failures, but as learning labs. Every tough exchange offers insight, into your clients, into recurring patterns, and into how you show up when it matters most.

Thoughts to carry forward

1. Emotional resilience helps advisors stay grounded and effective when facing skepticism, disengagement, or rejection during discovery meetings.

2. Techniques like intentional silence, reframing objections, and pausing before responding allow advisors to manage reactions in real time and build trust.

3. Long-term success depends on self-awareness, reflection, and developing habits that transform emotional challenges into stronger client relationships, and a more sustainable advisory practice.

27
THE POST-DISCOVERY PROCESS

Moving from Insight to Action

Keeping momentum alive after discovery

Discovery creates possibility. Follow-up determines what becomes of it. A great meeting may build connection, surface concerns, even spark hope, but it doesn't guarantee movement. What happens next, the tone you strike, the pace you set, the way you stay present without pressing, can shape whether that possibility turns into partnership or quietly fades into nothing.

Frequently, advisors lose momentum during this phase. Some follow up too quickly or too forcefully, which can feel like pressure. Others assume the prospect will reach out when ready and go silent, missing the chance to reinforce trust.

What to make of hesitation

You've wrapped up a strong discovery meeting. The rapport was real, the conversation flowed, and the concerns surfaced were meaningful. It's natural to expect momentum. But then: silence. No decision, no reply, no next step. It's easy to assume that prospects aren't interested. But more often, that silence isn't a "no." It's a pause, and that pause often carries more weight than it seems.

What feels like a standard meeting for the advisor might, for the prospect, represent the start of something major: retirement, inheritance, loss, or long-awaited transition. These moments don't always feel financial, they feel personal. And personal moments, especially high-stakes ones, are rarely followed by fast decisions.

Even when the meeting is energizing, the emotional load can leave a prospect mentally drained. Fatigue shows up not as disinterest but as hesitation. Some people need space to think. Others need time to feel their way through. They may be processing the facts while also seeking alignment with what feels emotionally and intuitively right.

That's where thoughtful follow-up becomes essential. Not to chase a decision, but to hold the connection. A timely check-in can help clarify emotions, reinforce trust, and gently guide the prospect back into the conversation. At their pace, not yours.

Silence is often reflection, not rejection

When you hear nothing after a discovery meeting, it's easy to assume the worst. But silence doesn't always mean indifference. More often, it means the prospect is still processing the conversation. They might be weighing the decision with a partner or sitting with the uncertainty that naturally arises when facing big financial questions.

In these moments, your role isn't to chase. It's to stay steady. To remain present, available, and quietly relevant without crossing into pressure. A well-timed follow-up can remind them of your presence, but what matters more is the tone. You're not nudging them toward a decision. You're signaling that the door remains open, and that trust, not urgency, is still the priority.

The 72-hour window: Why timing matters more than you think

Let's look at how timing shapes what comes next. The hours after a discovery meeting carry emotional momentum. The conversation is fresh, the questions are still resonating, and the prospect remains mentally engaged. But as time passes, that energy fades. Life resumes. Priorities shift. What once felt pressing now competes with everyday noise.

That's why the 48–72 hour window matters. Not to push, but to stay connected while the dialogue is still alive. Wait too long, and the opportunity dulls. Reach out too soon, and it can feel transactional.

The sweet spot lies in balance: a follow-up that feels timely, thoughtful, and grounded in the client's experience, not your agenda.

Structuring your follow-up: timing and tone

With timing in mind, how do you actually follow up in a way that supports trust?

Same-day follow-up (brief and personal):

- Thank them for the conversation
- Reflect one or two meaningful takeaways
- Express interest in continuing when the time is right

Three-day reconnect (low-pressure touchpoint):

- Ask how they've been feeling since the meeting
- Offer to clarify anything or revisit an earlier topic
- Keep it conversational, not persuasive

One-week value-add (relationship builder):

- Share a relevant article, resource, or story
- Reference a concern they shared to show attentiveness
- Ask an open-ended question to reopen dialogue

Why the 48–72 hour window works

A 48–72 hour follow-up keeps the momentum of the conversation alive while your insight is still top of mind. It's supported by both psychological insight and industry research. This timing aligns with the recency effect, a cognitive tendency for people to better recall recent experiences. Reconnecting while the conversation is still fresh helps sustain the emotional clarity and connection you created. It shows you're attentive and reinforces that their concerns are still on your radar.

From a practical perspective, this follow-up window keeps you visible without feeling intrusive. It balances responsiveness with respect for the prospect's decision-making process. When used thoughtfully, this rhythm strengthens engagement and lays a smoother path toward the next step.

Building confidence with subtle signals of social proof

After a meaningful conversation, it's natural for prospects to sit with lingering questions. Am I making the right choice? Is this the right person to guide me? While logic plays a role in decision-making, subtle reassurance often provides the final nudge. This is where social proof becomes quietly powerful. Not as a pitch, but as a soft signal that they're not navigating this alone.

Rather than listing credentials or accomplishments, share relatable experiences. You might say, "Many people I work with feel unsure about how much is enough for retirement. One couple felt the same. We walked through it together, and they left feeling much more confident about their next chapter." It's not about selling a solution. It's about reflecting shared experience.

Other cues can reinforce this trust as well: referencing a talk you gave, an article you wrote, or simply noting that you've worked with others facing similar questions. Even bringing in relevant research or broad trends can help prospects feel supported in their thinking. Used thoughtfully, social proof reassures the prospect they're not alone, and that their decision rests on familiar, steady ground.

When momentum stalls

Even the most promising conversations can go quiet. When that happens, the aim is not to push harder, but to gently reopen the door. A thoughtful, measured approach invites reengagement without creating pressure. Often, a simple message or a personal gesture is enough to remind the prospect that the conversation remains open, whenever they're ready to return. Flooding a prospect with more information rarely helps. It tends to overwhelm rather than clarify. And interpreting silence as a firm no can miss the mark. Often, they need more time, or a different kind of contact to reengage.

One of the most effective ways to follow up is with a simple, open message: "I trust you've had some time to reflect. I'm happy to pick things back up whenever it feels helpful." That kind of light touch communicates presence without pressure.

Sometimes, a more personal gesture makes the difference. A handwritten note, a short video message, or even a quick voicemail can stand out in a sea of templated follow-ups. These small signals carry weight because they feel real. Still, it's important to recognize that silence may sometimes be an answer in itself. Not every prospect is ready to move forward. Advisors who practice emotional intelligence know how to read the moment, when to lean in, and when to step back with grace.

Setting the stage for what comes next

The second meeting isn't a rehashed sales spiel. It's a continuation, a chance to revisit, clarify, and deepen the conversation. The most effective advisors plant that idea early, framing it gently during discovery with something like, "Most people find it helpful to have a second conversation to revisit questions before making any decisions." It signals openness without pressure.

When the time comes, that invitation can remain light and grounded: "Would it be helpful to go deeper on what we talked about?" There's no hard pivot, no rush. A steady, quiet signal that more is possible. And that you're ready to move forward when they are. In these moments, patience becomes a form of leadership.

As you close the first meeting, this is the time to reflect, not persuade. A simple line like, "Earlier, you mentioned feeling uncertain about whether your current plan can support the retirement you've envisioned," reinforces that you've been listening. From there, a check-in like, "How do you feel about everything we've discussed so far?" helps keep the conversation anchored in their experience.

When there's alignment, a thoughtful next step creates a smooth bridge: "Based on what I've heard, here's what I'd suggest we explore next." Calm, clear closure builds trust and helps the prospect leave with a sense of orientation, not obligation.

Thoughts to carry forward

1. A great discovery meeting is the starting point. Following up within 72 hours helps keep momentum strong and natural.

2. Emotional intelligence, timing, and subtle social proof help prospects feel understood, supported, and ready to move forward.

3. The best advisors don't *close*, they continue. Follow-up is a relationship move, not a sales move.

28
MOVING FROM CLARITY TO COMMITMENT

Helping Prospects Say Yes to Themselves

Bridging the gap between understanding and action

Your prospect understands what needs to be done. You've had a thoughtful conversation. They've asked good questions. You've explored their goals, fears, and priorities. And then, nothing. They don't say "Yes." They don't say "No." Only, "Let us think about it." And the momentum evaporates.

This is the moment many advisors find frustrating. The meeting felt good. There was connection, maybe even trust. But the next step doesn't happen. Not because your advice wasn't clear, or your discovery wasn't meaningful, but because something invisible, something internal, is slowing everything down.

This is a natural expression of how people respond in real conversations. People freeze in the face of complex decisions, especially when those decisions carry risk, uncertainty, or the threat of regret. Your prospect might be nodding in agreement, yet still unable to move. What they need now isn't more information. They need a way forward.

That's where your role deepens. Discovery isn't complete when clarity emerges. Discovery is complete when clarity becomes commitment. When the insight you've uncovered translates into action that moves them closer to what they want. This chapter is about building that bridge. Not with pressure. Not with persuasion. But with structure, empathy, and timing.

Why prospects pause, even when the path is clear

Every advisor has seen this: A prospect who feels engaged, even inspired, during the meeting, but then drifts into indecision afterward. Why?

Here are four common reasons:

1. Fear of commitment: Once a prospect takes action, they lose the psychological safety of "possibility." Committing means closing off other options. That can feel risky.

2. Present bias: Human brains overvalue short-term comfort over long-term gain. Even when the numbers make sense, "I'll deal with this later" is a powerful default.

3. Decision fatigue: Especially for prospects juggling multiple financial questions, one more decision can feel like too much. When the brain is tired, it avoids choices.

4. Loss aversion: People fear losing more than they value gaining. Even a well-framed recommendation can trigger the instinct to protect what they already have. These psychological factors aren't signs of resistance. They're signs of being human.

So the question becomes: how can you help your prospect navigate these invisible barriers without triggering pressure or fear?

Guidance without pressure: four ways to support forward motion

Advisors sometimes assume that time-bound proposals are sales tactics, tools to manufacture urgency. But they don't have to be. A time-bound proposal simply means attaching a decision or action to a meaningful point in time: like a tax deadline, a benefit window, or a personal milestone. When used ethically, these moments of timing become behavioral scaffolding. They support real decisions in real time, without pushing or pressuring. You're not closing a deal. You're guiding a person from "I get it" to "I'm ready."

That kind of guidance isn't about nudging people toward a yes. It's about creating the conditions for confident, grounded decisions. These four shifts create traction. They move prospects forward. With clarity, with care, and at the right pace.

First, anchor urgency in reality. Prospects are right to hesitate when they sense pressure from artificial deadlines. Trust grows when timing is based on something real: a tax-year cutoff, a policy nearing expiration, or a significant life event on the horizon. It's the difference between saying, "You should do this now," and pointing out, "If we get this in place before the end of the month, you'll be able to claim the deduction for this year." Or "Let's set up the 529 before your daughter's first birthday. Starting early gives you more years of compound growth." A real deadline doesn't apply pressure. It gives timing its proper context.

Second, translate impact into personal terms. Abstract urgency rarely resonates. But when the conversation ties directly to what someone values most, the shift is immediate. Smart timing plays a role, but the real aim is protecting what matters. For instance: "You told me your goal is to retire at 62 and spend more time traveling with your kids while they're still nearby.

Starting this Roth conversion now gives that goal a much better chance." Or "Every month we wait to fund this account, we lose compound growth. That could be $40,000 over 10 years. That's your grandson's college tuition." When urgency is personal, it becomes meaningful.

Third, break decisions into smaller, doable steps. People don't get stuck because they can't act—they get stuck because the next step feels too big. The solution is to shrink the moment. Say, "Let's start with the emergency fund. That's step one. Once that's in place, we'll revisit the rest." Or "Would it help to draft the documents now, with no signatures yet, so you have them ready when the time feels right?" Small yeses create forward motion.

Finally, maintain emotional safety. The bigger the decision, the more vulnerable it can feel. Prospects need to know the door doesn't slam behind them. Reassure them: "If something changes, we can always adapt. The important thing is to take a step that moves you forward." You're giving them psychological room to commit, without pressure, without fear. These shifts create space, space for clarity, choice, and forward motion. And in that space, decisions become easier to make, and easier to live with.

Five phrases that create momentum without pressure

When a prospect is on the edge of a decision, your words can either create resistance or open space. These five phrases keep the tone calm, clear, and collaborative, while gently moving things forward.

"You don't have to decide everything today. But let's take the next right step together."
Reduces overwhelm. Focuses the moment on movement.

"If this is something you want to benefit from this year, we'd need to start by [date]."
Ties action to real-world timing—no artificial urgency.

"Would it help to map out a decision timeline together?"
Transforms uncertainty into shared clarity.

"This opportunity aligns with what you told me matters most. Does it still feel like the right direction?"
Reconnects the decision to personal values.

"We can always revisit or fine-tune later. My focus is helping you take the step that best supports your goals."
Creates space. Reassures without retreating.

These aren't scripts. They're starting points. Simple phrases that invite progress, not pressure.

Commitment goes both ways

Even when prospects understand what to do, psychological barriers like fear, indecision, and loss aversion can hold them back. Advisors help turn insight into commitment not through pressure, but by offering structure, empathy, and manageable next steps.

But here's the parallel truth: prospects aren't the only ones who hesitate. Many advisors delay reaching out after a strong meeting, not because they don't know what to say, but because they're bracing for a response that feels personal. Ambivalence, hesitation, even a polite no can land like rejection. The silence feels ambiguous. Did something land wrong? Did the connection fade? Rather than risk hearing no, they wait.

The cost isn't always immediate. It's cumulative: misfit clients, lost opportunities, and a practice that slowly drifts off course.

And even when you do everything right, some prospects still won't move forward. Not because you failed, but because they can't, or won't, take the next step. That's not a signal to keep chasing. It's a signal to move on. Focus your energy where there's real engagement. As the saying goes: *"Some will. Some won't. So what."*

These conversations go both ways. You're not there to win everyone. You're there to choose the right fit. You're shaping the future of your practice. "Doing well enough" can quietly become the enemy of doing your best work. The clients you attract, the stories they bring, the values they prioritize, everything begins with how you show up in discovery. That's the difference the advisor makes. And that's why commitment belongs on both sides of the table.

Thoughts to carry forward

1. Even when prospects appear clear, psychological barriers like fear, indecision, and loss aversion often block action. Understanding alone doesn't drive action.

2. Advisors can guide prospects forward not with pressure, but by offering real-world timing, personal relevance, small next steps, and emotional safety.

3. Commitment is a two-way street: advisors must be willing to follow up with courage, and willing to walk away when the fit isn't there.

29

HOW DISCOVERY DRIVES REFERRALS AND RETENTION

Trust That Multiplies

Turning great conversations into loyalty and referrals

Advisors often treat referrals and retention as separate goals. But both begin in the same place: the first real conversation. A great discovery meeting does more than collect information. It creates connection. It builds trust. It sparks commitment. When clients feel truly heard, they're more likely to stay, and more inclined to share that experience with others. Discovery becomes the engine behind both loyalty and advocacy.

Why some clients refer, and why some won't

Many advisors assume happy clients will refer. But satisfaction alone isn't enough. Referrals are emotional, driven by trust and a desire to help. A personalized, insightful discovery process helps clients feel personally known. When clients feel emotionally connected, they're more likely to share the experience. Sometimes it's out of gratitude. Sometimes pride. Sometimes the simple impulse to be helpful. Referrals often come from a sense of reciprocity or social connection.

Not every satisfied client will refer. Some are private, hesitant, or think you're too busy. That's fine. Referrals start with how someone feels after the first meeting. Even a few passionate clients can become a steady source of introductions, if the experience is worth sharing.

Discovery drives loyalty

Discovery is more than onboarding. It's the moment a prospect decides whether you're someone they can trust for the long haul. When that meeting feels rushed or overly transactional, you blend into the crowd. At first, you're another provider. One of many. But when you slow down and ask about values, fears, and long-term hopes, the dynamic changes. You step into the role of a confidant.

Yes, results matter. Clients care about performance, accuracy, and follow-through. But those things alone don't build loyalty. What keeps people coming back is emotional security. The sense that their advisor sees them, hears them, and remembers what matters. A strong discovery process uncovers both goals and barriers early. It signals care, foresight, and leadership. And that's what turns an initial conversation into a lasting relationship.

Ask better questions. Move beyond the data. Explore what matters most: values, transitions, priorities. Then listen, fully and without rushing to solve. Often, the most meaningful thing you can offer is not advice, but attention. Clients remember being heard. And don't treat discovery as a one-time event. Revisit the deeper questions regularly. As life evolves, so do goals and priorities. Continued discovery signals that your care runs deeper than the surface.

That's what leads to referable moments. Not from referral drives or polished campaigns, but from something real. When an advisor remembers a wedding anniversary and sends a handwritten card, that moment resonates. It becomes a story the client wants to share. When discovery is meaningful, it becomes memorable. And that's what fuels organic, lasting growth.

Thoughts to carry forward

1. A strong discovery process builds emotional trust and personal connection, making clients more likely to stay long-term and refer others.

2. Not every client will refer, but a small group of enthusiastic advocates can drive consistent introductions when the experience feels genuinely worth sharing

3. Improving discovery, through deeper questions, active listening, and ongoing conversations, leads to stronger relationships, fewer issues, and greater business growth.

30

YOUR INFLECTION POINT

Change is Calling

What if you do nothing?

Let's say you keep doing what's always worked. The process holds. Clients sign up. The calendar stays full. On the surface, everything looks fine. But here's what we've seen when advisors don't evolve their discovery process.

They keep working hard, but the spark begins to dim. Clients still come, but the energy fades. Joy and engagement slip quietly out the back door. They start saying yes to clients who aren't a fit. It's rarely about being difficult. More often, it's a mismatch in values or timing. The cost isn't always financial. Sometimes it shows up as frustration, or a subtle resentment that lingers after meetings.

And they miss the clients they truly want to serve. Not because they lack the skill, but because they never reached the depth of connection those clients were seeking. It doesn't unravel all at once. There's no breaking point. It starts with a slow drift. Almost invisible at first, until one day, the work doesn't feel like yours anymore.

Somewhere along the way, success lost its shape. And meanwhile, the financial landscape is already shifting. Quietly, but definitively. This isn't the edge of transformation. It's already underway, and the data shows it.

Women will soon control much of the wealth

By 2030, women in the U.S. are projected to control approximately $34 trillion in investable assets, representing about 38% of the nation's total. That shift is already underway, driven by inheritance through the *Great Wealth Transfer*, increased longevity as women outlive men and inherit spousal wealth, and rising empowerment as more women become primary earners and financial decision-makers. They're values-driven, purpose-oriented, and collaborative. What they're looking for is guidance that speaks to their whole life, not only their finances. They look for trusted partnerships that support meaningful decisions over time.

Younger generations expect more

Millennials and Gen Z grew up saturated with information. They don't need someone to explain the markets. They need help making sense of the noise.

They come asking: Can I count on this person? Do they get me? Do they respect my autonomy?

They're discerning, shaped by experience and quick to recognize what's genuine. A discovery process rooted in rapport, emotional intelligence, and co-creation isn't a soft skill. It's your strategy for staying relevant.

AI is fast. You are human. That's the difference.

The rise of AI isn't theoretical. It's happening now. Today's AI can generate personalized financial plans, parse and analyze tax documents, anticipate spending habits and portfolio gaps, and simulate retirement scenarios in seconds. Very soon, it will outperform humans in the logistics of discovery: intake forms, diagnostics, even surface-level personalization.

So, what's left for you? Everything that matters. Warmth, empathy, the courage to sit in silence and let someone else speak first, the ability to catch what wasn't said and follow the thread. It's the human ability to turn facts into trust and numbers into meaning. AI can't feel. It can't connect. It can't earn trust in the middle of a story about a mother's illness or a child's fear of money. That's not algorithmic. That's human.

The tipping point

You're standing at the edge of a decision. On one side is what's familiar. Comfort, habit, the processes that have worked well enough until now. On the other is something more open-ended. Evolution. Curiosity. The chance to build a practice that feels as good on the inside as it looks on paper. You don't have to burn everything down. But you do need a new blueprint.

Is your discovery process built for the kind of clients you want to serve next? Would you hire yourself if you were a 32-year-old woman managing a $2 million inheritance? Are you coasting on what worked last year? Or building for the clients you haven't met yet? Comfort is efficient. But it rarely breaks new ground.

Because every discovery conversation is more than a step in your process. It's a turning point, for the prospect and for you. Every question you ask, every moment of attention you give, is shaping the future of your practice. The older model focused on telling. On control. On getting through the pitch. The emerging model does something else. It listens first. It collaborates. It begins with, "What really matters to you?" and builds from there.

We're in the midst of a shift that's changing the advisor-client relationship from the ground up. How it begins, how it grows, how it holds. It's a deeper shift, in how trust is built, in how advice is delivered, and in what clients are coming to expect. They've already moved forward. The only real question is whether your process has kept up.

Here's why that matters

There's a quiet irony at the heart of this shift: the changes that make the biggest difference are often simple, even obvious. They don't require reinvention, only intention. Most advisors aren't doing this. The barrier isn't ability, it's comfort. The old way still carries them forward, so they stay with it.

That's exactly what creates your advantage. We estimate that more than 90 percent of advisors are not practicing the foundational behaviors described in this book. If you choose to act on them, you will immediately set yourself apart from the 300,000 other financial advisors.

Common sense isn't common practice. The discovery shift invites you to show up differently, fully present, deeply attuned, and willing to lead with courage instead of performance. When you do, you stand out without trying to. That is the work that separates advisors who adapt from those who fade. The future isn't approaching. It has arrived. And it's yours to shape.

Final Note

What you carry forward

Discovery Shift isn't a checklist. It's a compass.

Keep it close. Revisit it when the conversation slips into habit. Or when you forget what this work is really about.

- Talk less than you want to.
- Ask fewer questions, but better ones.
- Make room for silence.
- Tune your ear to more than answers. Listen for what's driving them.
- Warmth builds trust faster than credentials.
- Resist the impulse to over-clarify.
- Don't take a nod as proof they're fine.
- It's not about what you uncover. It's about what they feel safe enough to share.
- Clarity before commitment. Presence before pitch.
- You don't have to impress them. You have to see them.

You don't need to master all of this at once. Start with one practice. Then build from there.

That's how this work can change you.

That's how you become unforgettable.

About the Author

Chris Holman, MCC, began his career in 1981, dialing strangers at EF Hutton with nothing more than a phone and persistence. He rose to become national director of investments for a $10 billion firm, but his real fascination was never the markets, it was people. What makes someone say yes to a stranger with a business card and a promise? That question has driven his work for more than four decades.

In the early 2000s, he began sharing insights through The *Prospecting Professor*, one of the industry's first advisor-focused blogs. Since 2007, Chris has coached more than 2,500 financial advisors, drawing on both his years in the trenches and his research into how advisors connect and build trust. He is also the founder of the Discovery Meeting Workshop, the industry's only research-based training that helps advisors transform their approach and add new clients with greater ease and efficiency.

Today, as executive coach at Horsesmouth and a Master Certified Coach with the International Coach Federation, Chris helps advisors sharpen their discovery process, deepen conversations, and win clients by listening.

A San Francisco native whose great-great-grandfather arrived during the 1849 Gold Rush, Chris has lived in Minneapolis since 1979. He welcomes comments and can be reached at **cholman@horsesmouth.com**.

Horsesmouth

Horsesmouth helps financial professionals educate their clients and grow their businesses. We serve advisors, planners, agents, accountants, and other financial services professionals with practical strategies, training, and resources designed to help them become more effective and successful advisors.

Horsesmouth's flagship service delivers daily business development, practice management, and financial planning guidance to help professionals stay ahead in a rapidly changing industry. Many also rely on *Advisor/Client*, our year-round program for marketing and client communications that makes it easier to reach, engage, and retain clients.

Financial professionals across the country turn to Horsesmouth's Savvy client education programs, which help them build technical skills while educating their clients and communities on life's most important financial decisions. The best known is the industry-leading *Savvy Social Security Planning®* program, which equips advisors to help clients take their first steps toward comprehensive retirement planning.

Horsesmouth also offers in-depth workshops that provide technical expertise while building related business development and practice management skills. These include the *Savvy Tax Planning School for Financial Advisors*, *The Financial Educator Marketing Workshop*, and *The Discovery Meeting Workshop* series.

Horsesmouth is headquartered in New York City and has been serving financial professionals since 1996.

Index

www.ingramcontent.com/pod-product-compliance
Lightning Source LLC
Chambersburg PA
CBHW060041030426
42334CB00019B/2434